EXPLORING OCEAN ECOSYSTEMS

CURRICULUM GUIDE

Project manager: *Gerald E. Marino*
Editorial: *Tara McCarthy, Hilarie Staton*
Graphic design: *Eldon P. Slick and Maurene Mongan*
Science investigations and strategies: *Julie Kane Brinkmann, M.S.*
Science consultant and instructional design: *Debra Miners*
Production manager*: Christine Bateman*
Editorial production: *Renee Burch, Marjorie Shaw, Dana Monroe*

Printed in the United States of America

Exploring Ocean Ecosystems
ISBN # 0-937934-93-3

Published by Wildlife Education, Ltd.®
9820 Willow Creek Rd., Suite 300
San Diego, CA 92131-1112

EXPLORING OCEAN ECOSYSTEMS

Table of Contents

EXPLORING OCEAN ECOSYSTEMS

UNIT 1
Ocean Ecosystems

The ocean ecosystems have unique characteristics.

- They contain wide varieties of living and nonliving things.
- Each contains a variety of habitats that support living things.
- The living things interact in an ocean environment to meet their needs.
- The living things form a food web through which energy flows throughout the ocean ecosystems.

UNIT 2
Animal Adaptations

Ocean animals have structural and behavioral adaptations that enable them to meet their needs.

- They have adaptations for obtaining food and oxygen.
- They have adaptations to help themselves and their young survive in salt water.
- They have adaptations to protect themselves from predators.

UNIT 3
Humans and the Ocean Ecosystems

Humans are interdependent parts of the ocean ecosystems.

- We depend on the ocean for many of our needs.
- Our interaction with ocean ecosystems affects the living and nonliving parts of the ocean.
- We have the responsibility to ensure that our actions do not harm the ocean ecosystems.

⊤HE ZOOBOOKS® PROGRAM

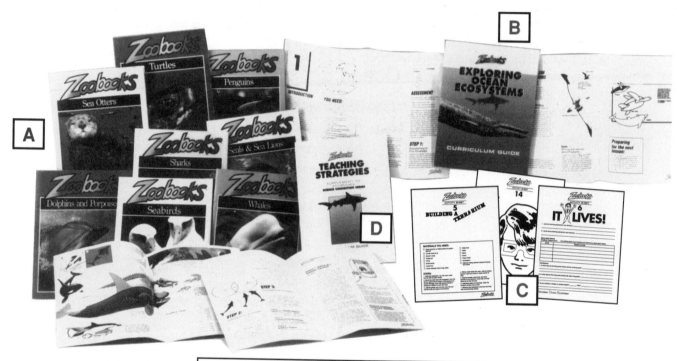

Each *Zoobooks* Teaching Module Consists Of

A Multiple copies of each *Zoobooks* title in the module

B A Curriculum Guide

C Reproducible student Activity Sheets (included in the Curriculum Guide)

D A *Teaching Strategies* Supplement with hints, help, and ideas to carry out the suggested activities and learning experiences.

ZOOBOOKS, with their magazine format, vivid illustrations, and inviting captions and text, have long appealed to children lucky enough to subscribe to them at home. In addition, parents and other educators appreciate *Zoobooks* for the accuracy of their content, the depth of their treatment, and the way in which they make scientific language accessible to young readers.

Now the *Zoobooks,* coupled with teaching guides, have been clustered into modules for classroom use. Each *Zoobooks* teaching module uses the thematic treatment recommended by recent statewide framework guidelines and by Project 2061. The modules enable your students to use *Zoobooks* to explore related science concepts in depth. They help you to supplement your science curriculum with exciting, hands-on activities and extend and apply science concepts in other areas of your curriculum.

EXPLORING OCEAN ECOSYSTEMS

This teaching module, "EXPLORING OCEAN ECOSYSTEMS," tells the story of an ecosystem and how humans interact with it. Ocean ecosystems are used as the specific example, but the concepts explored run through all ecosystems.

The eight *Zoobooks* titles in this module are:

Sharks
Seals and Sea Lions
Seabirds
Dolphins and Porpoises
Sea Otters
Penguins
Whales
Turtles

The module consists of ten lessons, which are grouped in three units.

Unit 1: Ocean Ecosystems
Unit 2: Animal Adaptations
Unit 3: Humans and the Ocean Ecosystems

The Ocean Ecosystems module unfolds like this:

Unit 1 defines an ecosystem and describes its components and characteristics. Through observation of an artificial classroom ecosystem that students create, they learn how animals interact within their ecosystems. They also discover how energy is transferred throughout an ecosystem as living things acquire and share resources with others to meet their collective survival needs.

Unit 2 explores animal adaptations and how different species have adapted to survive in an ecosystem. Structural and behavioral adaptations are demonstrated and investigated through simulations, games, and classroom projects.

Unit 3 examines how humans depend on and interact with ocean ecosystems. Through simulations of "City Council" meetings and TV news exposé shows, the complex web of our dependence on our oceans is revealed.

Time: In most classrooms, each lesson will take two to three weeks.

Your Options: Adapt the module to your curriculum and your students' interests and needs. For example, if you're concentrating on the ocean this year, you may want to use all the lessons sequentially. If you're concentrating on animal adaptations, you may want to select Unit 2 for a focus. If your students are involved in a month-long study of environmental concerns, you can use Unit 1 and/or Unit 3 to enrich and extend their understanding.

STRATEGIES FOR LEARNING

The *Zoobooks* format supports outcome-based education. The module's design allows for adaptation to your school's specific curriculum. It also empowers teachers to use their skills, experience, and knowledge in directing and enhancing student learning.

Students approach and explore concepts through a variety of activities which are designed to appeal to their different learning modalities. They solve problems and reach conclusions through simulation games, cooperative learning activities, and investigations that call for manipulative skills. They are invited to extend and apply their science skills and understanding in stimulating and highly relevant interdisciplinary activities.

AUTHENTIC ASSESSMENT

Evaluation is an ongoing process. *Zoobooks* modules provide several real-life strategies to help you and your students assess progress and evaluate outcomes. These include:

- Cooperative learning activities
- Unit projects
- Student portfolios and journals
- Hands-on science investigations and record keeping
- Student-developed criteria

iii

USING THE MODULE TO BUILD READING SKILLS

Through *Zoobooks,* students have an opportunity to transfer skills learned in your reading instruction to a wide variety of trade books, magazines, resource books, and other reading materials. Along the way, in many of the lessons, reviews of reading and study strategies are suggested. In addition, you may wish to introduce the module by going over one of the *Zoobooks* with the class to point out the different components that are to be read and integrated, such as titles, main text, captions, and visuals (panoramas, cross-sections, diagrams, graphs and charts).

While most students are familiar with these devices through their prior use of magazines, encyclopedias, and other reference materials, you should provide extra help for students who have difficulty integrating ideas from these different presentations. Here are some suggestions:

• In a small group, review reading and study strategies as often as necessary. Invite students in the group to discuss any problems they have encountered and how they are solving them. Ask these students to help you make a Reading Strategies chart to display in the classroom.

• As students with special needs work in heterogeneous cooperative groups, intercede as needed to make sure they are (1) using their strengths, and (2) not holding up other members of the group. In this latter case, provide special-needs students with related tasks that are not so time-bound, yet contribute to the group's overall task, such as working at the word processor or reviewing books and other material presented at a level they have mastered.

• Because students have different learning styles and modalities, allow them to use their strongest or preferred learning style in their projects, reports, and activities. For instance, you could allow a student to substitute an oral or video presentation in places where a written presentation is indicated.

Or you might have a student use visual and graphic skills to represent something that you would expect other students to complete in written form.

LESSON STRUCTURE

Each lesson in the *Zoobooks* module is made up of five constant steps that help students attain the objectives stated at the beginning of the lesson.

STEP 1:
Brainstorming for Prior Knowledge

These discussions foster a "can-do" attitude in students by showing them what they already know about the lesson topic and enabling them to suggest the problem they will solve next and predict various outcomes. Brainstorming also acts as an informal pre-assessment, showing what students already know, exposing misconceptions, and highlighting students' interests.

STEP 2:
Defining Terms

Through class discussion, students help to develop a working definition of one or two key words that are integral to understanding the lesson content and concept.

STEP 3:
Investigation

This is an exploration that involves students interactively with the science concepts. Students learn the concept through hands-on investigations or simulation activities.

(All of these use inexpensive, easy-to-find materials.) Students evaluate what they have learned through follow-up discussion and further applications of the concept.

STEP 4:
Cooperative Learning

Students form cooperative learning groups that are maintained throughout the unit. In each lesson, the groups have specific tasks to accomplish that require them to implement what they learned in the investigation, then share the outcome with the class.

STEP 5:
Unit Project

Students choose a project to complete by the end of the unit. They can work on their projects individually, with a partner, or with a group. The unit projects serve two major purposes: (1) They provide a hands-on way for students to integrate the "big ideas" of the unit into a meaningful whole that they can share with classmates; (2) They provide students with an authentic assessment device through which they can evaluate what they have learned. Step 5 in each lesson suggests how students can enrich their projects with that lesson's discoveries.

ECOCONNECTION ACTIVITY

The Ecoconnection Activity provides activities that apply the lesson concepts to the aquarium or terrarium which students set up in your classroom, or to the mini-ecosystem in your area. Thus, students are encouraged to apply the concepts to a miniature ecosystem. Appropriate miniature ecosystems include an area on the playground, a nearby wildlife area, or students' backyards.

CURRICULUM CONNECTIONS

The Curriculum Connections that end each lesson suggest activities to expand your interdisciplinary classroom. Students can use the content and concepts from their science activities to enrich their appreciation of literature, to build their geography skills, to enhance their social studies understanding, to appreciate the role of mathematics as it is used by scientists, and to inspire creative work in writing, art, and music. In turn, the students' experiences in these areas build their science skills and knowledge.

OTHER LESSON COMPONENTS
Activity Sheets

Virtually every lesson has one or more reproducible Activity Sheets. These serve different purposes, and their use is described and keyed in each lesson. Some sheets provide charts or diagrams to be used with one or another of the five lesson steps. Others provide a stimulus or a worksheet for a Curriculum Connection activity.

Student Portfolios

The *Teaching Strategies* Supplement suggests ways to help students build portfolios as they work through each unit. As you know, individual portfolios help students enhance and organize learning, encourage them to develop criteria for good academic work, provide authentic portraits of the student as a learner, and provide a way for students to analyze and assess their work.

Portfolios developed in conjunction with *Zoobooks* units can include the following:

- Glossaries
- Results of investigations
- Results of cooperative learning activities
- Activity Sheets
- Curriculum Connections activities

v

- Journals, logs, or other written materials or graphics that record the students' ideas, questions, and conclusions.

From time to time, you may wish to have students work with a learning partner to refine and assess their portfolios' contents. You might also schedule portfolio conferences to provide reinforcement and encouragement and to help students set realistic criteria for themselves by which they can assess their progress. Sample Student Goal Sheets and Student-Teacher Conference Sheets are included in your *Teaching Strategies* Supplement.

ADDITIONAL RESOURCES FOR THE OCEAN ECOSYSTEMS MODULE

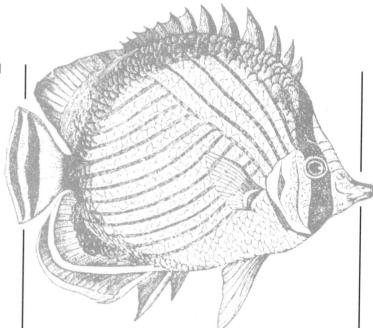

To help build their skills of thinking and working as scientists do, students need a rich variety of resource materials. In addition to the *Zoobooks,* general and nature encyclopedias, and materials about the ocean and ocean animals borrowed from your library, you may want to provide students with access to some of the following references. (Target audience age is in parentheses.)

Periodicals

1. *Current Science* (11 and above). Bimonthly news magazine covering latest developments in science and technology. (3001 Cindel Drive, P.O. Box 8996, Delran, NJ 08370-8996)

2. *Dolphin Log* (7–15). Bimonthly magazine bringing together various disciplines as they relate to the global water system. (The Cousteau Society, 870 Greenbriar Circle, Suite 402, Chesapeake, VA 23320)

3. *National Geographic World* (8–14). Monthly magazine featuring factual stories about natural history and science. (*National Geographic World*, 1145 17th Street, NW, Washington, DC 20036)

4. *Owl Magazine* (8–13). 10-issues-a-year magazine dealing with late-breaking news about science, animals, and technology. (*Owl Magazine*, 56 The Esplanade, Suite 306, Toronto, Ontario M5E 1A7 Canada)

5. *Ranger Rick* (6–12). Monthly magazine using photo/caption stories and personalized adventures of animals. (National Wildlife Federation, 8925 Leesburg Pike, Vienna, VA 22180-0001)

Sources for Additional Activity and Teaching Ideas

1. Water, Precious Water—Project AIMS. A Collection of Elementary Water Activities. (AIMS Education Foundation, P.O. Box 8120, Fresno, CA 93747-8120)

2. Marine Ecology and Conservation (Grades K–3 or ages 4–8). $5.00. (Sea World Education Department, 1720 South Shore Road, San Diego, CA 92109)

Materials for a Technology-Based Learning Center

(Using Apple IIe and IIgs Computers)

1. Animal Watch: Whales. Students can create and print original books from the software's scenes. Five copies of a booklet come with the package. (Learningways Explore-a-Science Series, D.C. Heath. Distributed by William K. Bradford, 310 School Street, Acton, MA 01720)

2. Bank Street School Filer (also available for Commodore 64). Students can use this to create an ocean animal database for access by classmates. (Sunburst Communications, 101 Castleton Street, Pleasantville, NY 10570)

3. Deluxe Paint II. Students can use this full-fledged paint program to create digitalized images, then use the finished images to illustrate their journals or to add to their portfolios. (Electronic Arts, 1450 Fashion Island Boulevard, San Mateo, CA 94404)

(Using IBM-Compatible Computers)

1. Windows Draw. Another full-range paint program, but made for IBM-compatible computers. (Micrografx® Inc., 1303 Arapaho, Richardson, TX 75081)

UNIT 1

The Ocean Ecosystems

Unit Concept:

THE OCEAN ECOSYSTEMS HAVE UNIQUE CHARACTERISTICS.

- *They contain wide varieties of living and nonliving things.*

- *Each contains a variety of habitats that support living things.*

- *The living things interact in an ocean environment to meet their needs.*

- *The living things form a food web through which energy flows throughout the ocean ecosystems.*

LESSON

1

INTRODUCING OCEANS AND ECOSYSTEMS

The ocean contains wide varieties of living and nonliving things.

INTRODUCTION

Students explore the living and nonliving components of an ecosystem by creating and observing their own ecosystem or seeking out an existing one. They do this by (1) setting up and observing a seawater or a freshwater aquarium, (2) building a terrarium, or (3) exploring a mini-ecosystem in their city (such as an area on the playground, a nearby wildlife area, or an area in students' backyards). They then form cooperative learning groups that will study the ecosystem of the specific animal their group's *Zoobook* covers. Students begin their unit project by examining a particular aspect of an ocean ecosystem, which they will continue to study throughout the unit. For additional information to facilitate the procedure and to enhance students' learning, see "TEACHER'S NOTES AND BACKGROUND INFORMATION" on page 11.

OBJECTIVES:

1. To investigate the components of an ecosystem
2. To identify the characteristics of some living things in the ocean ecosystem

YOU NEED:

1. Copies of the eight *Zoobooks* in this module
2. For the science investigation:
   - **Choose 1:**
     For the Seawater Aquarium,
     copies of Activity Sheets 1 and 2
         or
     For the Freshwater Aquarium,
     copies of Activity Sheets 3 and 4
         or
     For the Terrarium,
     copies of Activity Sheets 5 and 6
         or
     For the Mini-Ecosystem Observation,
     copies of Activity Sheet 7
   - materials to build an aquarium or terrarium (See Activity Sheets 1, 3, and 5)
3. For the cooperative learning activity, copies of Activity Sheet 8 (two sheets)
4. Reference materials
5. Writing and art materials

LESSON OUTLINE

Before the lesson begins:

Based on your available resources and goals, decide whether your students will work with a seawater aquarium, a freshwater aquarium, a

EXPLORING OCEAN ECOSYSTEMS

terrarium, or a mini-ecosystem in the area. Information to help you decide which activity is correct for you can be found on pages 5-7. For whatever activity you select for your class to do

1. (a) Collect the materials needed to set up seawater aquarium(s) in the classroom
    or
    (b) Collect the materials needed for a freshwater aquarium
    or
    (c) Collect the materials needed for a terrarium
    or
    (d) have a parent or pet store donate aquarium or terrarium materials
    or
    (e) select a mini-ecosystem in its natural setting to study in your city
2. Prepare the Activity Sheets and *Zoobooks* used in the lesson.
3. Have students complete the assessment activity.

During the lesson:

1. Follow the lesson steps to have students
    (a) Brainstorm for prior knowledge of an ecosystem.
    (b) Define the term ECOSYSTEM.
    (c) Perform the science investigation to create an ecosystem and observe its components.
    (d) Break up into cooperative learning groups and complete the appropriate Activity Sheet to describe the ecosystem of the animal they are studying.
    (e) Begin their unit projects. (**Note:** When you discuss the concept of unit projects with students, develop criteria with them to evaluate those projects. Refer to the *Teaching Strategies* Supplement for how to do this.)
2. Have students start their <u>Ocean Ecosystems Portfolios</u>, which they will add to during the entire unit.
3. Direct students to look for and collect material from magazines, newspapers, and other reading sources that give information about current topics concerning the world's oceans.

4. Have students select reading material that they will read during the unit. They can find titles listed in the bibliography or other appropriate places such as the library.
5. Direct students to begin their Ocean Journals.
6. Words to add to your **Classroom Glossary:**

    Community
    Ecology
    Ecosystem
    Environment
    Living
    Nonliving
    System

PRE- AND POST-ASSESSMENT

Have students fold a sheet of paper into three sections and label the three sections as

1. What I know about the ocean.
2. What I'd like to learn about the ocean.
3. What I've discovered about the ocean.

Have students fill in the first two sections and collect them for your review before you begin the lesson. Use them to determine what students already know and what their strengths are, as well as what they don't know or what misconceptions they have about the topic. These pre-assessments may be useful to help students select topics for their unit projects. Return them to students and have them store them in their portfolios. When the unit is complete, have students fill in the third section ("What I've discovered about the ocean") detailing what they have learned in the unit. Since this is Unit 1's culminating activity, more information on completing this section appears at the end of Lesson 4.

STEP 1:

Brainstorming for Prior Knowledge

Distribute the *Zoobooks* to small groups of students. Invite them to browse through the books

and predict what the unit as a whole is about. Then review with students the fact that the ocean covers about 72% of the Earth's surface. Invite students to name characteristics of the ocean that they know about through personal experience, through previous study, or through examining a globe. Ask students to compare and contrast the ocean with freshwater lakes, rivers, and ponds. Write their ideas on the chalkboard. You might set up a Venn diagram like the one below as a device for identifying shared and unique features. Conclude the brainstorming by inviting students to list questions they hope the unit will answer about the ocean and about the animals in the *Zoobooks*. Keep the list on display.

4

STEP 2:
Defining Terms: Ecosystem

Write ECOSYSTEM on the chalkboard and discuss the two parts of the word. "Eco-" is from the Greek "oikos," house or home. Invite students to suggest a broad meaning for eco- in a word with which they are familiar, such as ecology, where eco- refers to environment. Students can then discuss the word "system" as it is used in terms like <u>circulatory system</u>, <u>railway system</u>, and <u>social system</u>: a group of parts or elements that act together and depend upon one another to make up a whole. Ask students to hypothesize,

then check in a dictionary for a definition of the word <u>ecosystem</u>. Possibilities: (1) All living and nonliving things in a given area and the relationships among them; (2) An ecological community together with its environment. Students may be able to give examples of ecosystems they have already studied, such as desert or forest ecosystems.

A PROBLEM TO SOLVE: Write the following question on poster paper for display: *"What are the components of an ocean ecosystem?"* Explain that as students work through this unit they will gather material that will help them to solve this problem. They might make a related generalization about components that apply to any ecosystem. Suggest that students begin their solutions by writing down the class's definition of ecosystem and making notes based on the brainstorming activity about the ocean.

STEP 3:
Investigating an Ecosystem

Estimated time: 2 weeks

This investigation enables students to create a mini-ecosystem which they will observe throughout the *Zoobooks* module. An ecoconnection activity at the end of each lesson challenges students to apply the lesson concepts to their aquarium, terrarium, or mini-ecosystem. The directions below allow teacher flexibility in choosing a mini-ecosystem that best meets their classroom needs and environment.

Choice 1:
Setting up a Seawater Aquarium
Students compare variables in seawater to determine its properties and create a seawater environment hospitable to aquatic life.

Choice 2:
Creating a Freshwater Aquarium
Students observe and compare temperature and pH in freshwater to create a suitable habitat for freshwater plants and animals.

Choice 3:
Building a Terrarium
Students use a variety of materials to build a terrarium.

Choice 4: Observing a local Mini-ecosystem
Students observe the living and nonliving components of a mini-ecosystem at school or at home.

1. Setting up a Seawater Aquarium

Procedure:
1. Explain that students will be working in groups of five or six to investigate the properties of seawater and factors that cause it to change. As students investigate these properties, they will experiment with the properties to create a seawater environment that will support aquatic life.

Show students the empty aquarium. Ask students to identify all of the living and nonliving parts they will need to add to create a seawater ecosystem (seawater, oxygen, plants, animals, sand or gravel, etc.). Write temperature, salinity/density, and pH on the board next to the students' list. Explain that these are factors of the seawater which must be in a correct range to support life. Explain each of these terms and demonstrate the tools and methods for measuring each factor. Ask each group to decide which one they will investigate. Tell students the ranges of each element that are necessary to enable living things to survive in the ecosystem.

Temperature: 40-70 degrees F (ideal is 52-55 degrees F); Density: 1.0230-1.0245; pH: 7.5-8.3. (Note: Check with your pet supplier to determine the ideal ranges for the specific organisms you plan to use.)

2. Distribute Activity Sheet 1 and have students assist you in preparing the aquarium. Prepare the seawater according to Step 2 in "TEACHER'S NOTES AND BACKGROUND INFORMATION" on page 11, or ask student volunteers to help you with this preparation.

3. Ask the class to decide where to place the aquarium to begin the investigation. After one week, change the location or another variable to see how it affects pH, density, or temperature.

4. Distribute Activity Sheet 2 and ask groups to use it to record measurable and/or visual changes in the aquarium over a two-week period.

5. At the end of two weeks, ask each group to present its findings and conclusions to the class.

Conclusion:
1. Encourage the class to discuss relationships of variables, such as filtration to oxygen, or pH to temperature.

2. Ask students to decide, on the basis of all the investigations, whether seawater, i.e., the ocean, is a simple entity or a complex one, and to give reasons for their decision.

3. Once students have created an environment with the correct ranges for temperature, salinity, and pH, they can introduce a crab or other living animals or plants to the aquarium. Students should continue to monitor the aquarium to ensure the environment will support life.

2. Creating a Freshwater Aquarium

Procedure:
1. Explain that students will be working in groups of five or six to investigate the properties of freshwater and factors that cause it to change. As

5

students investigate these properties, they will experiment with the properties to create a freshwater environment that will support aquatic life. Ask students to identify all of the living and nonliving parts they will need to add to create a freshwater ecosystem (freshwater, oxygen, plants, animals, sand or gravel, etc.). Write temperature and pH on the board next to the students' list. Explain that these are factors of the freshwater which must be in a correct range to support life. Explain each of these terms and demonstrate the tools and methods for measuring each factor. Ask each group to decide which one they will investigate. Tell students the ranges of each element that are necessary to enable living things to survive in the ecosystem.

Temperature: 40-70 degrees F (ideal is 52-55 degrees F); pH: 7.5-8.3. (Note: Check with your pet supplier to determine the ideal ranges for the specific organisms you plan to use.)

2. Distribute Activity Sheet 3 and have students assist you in preparing the aquarium. Prepare the freshwater according to Step 2, or ask student volunteers to help you with this preparation.

3. Ask the class to decide where to place the aquarium to begin the investigation. After one week, change the location or another variable to see how it affects pH or temperature.

4. Distribute Activity Sheet 4 and ask groups to use it to record measurable and/or visual changes in the aquarium over a two-week period.

5. At the end of two weeks, ask each group to present its findings and conclusions to the class.

Conclusion:

1. Encourage the class to discuss relationships of variables, such as filtration to oxygen, or pH to temperature.

2. Ask students to decide, on the basis of all the investigations, whether freshwater, i.e., their water ecosystem, is a simple entity or a complex one, and to give reasons for their decision.

3. Once students have created an environment with the correct ranges for temperature and pH, they can introduce a fish or other living animals or plants to the aquarium. Students should continue to monitor the aquarium to ensure the environment will support life.

3. Building a Terrarium

Procedure:

1. Tell students that they will be using materials to create their own mini-ecosystem in a terrarium. Show students the terrarium container (aquarium, jar, liter soda bottle) and ask them to brainstorm a list of materials which could go into the terrarium (soil, air, water, plants, animals).

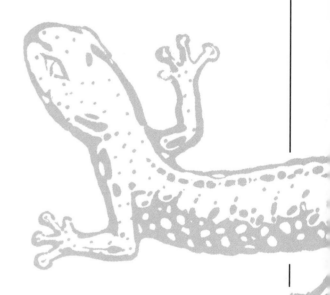

2. Distribute Activity Sheet 5 and assist students in building their terrariums.

3. Place the terrariums in a convenient location and allow students to make observations over a two-week period. Students can record observations on Activity Sheet 6.

Conclusion:

1. Encourage the class to discuss their observations.

2. Ask students to decide, on the basis of all the investigations, whether a terrarium ecosystem is a simple entity or a complex one, and to give reasons for their decision.

6

4. Observing a Local Mini-Ecosystem

Procedure:

1. Take students to the mini-ecosystem or assign for homework by telling students to find a mini-ecosystem in their yards or a nearby wildlife area. Tell students that they will be observing the mini-ecosystem to identify its living and nonliving parts and the ways these parts affect each other.

2. Distribute Activity Sheet 7 and assist students in writing their observations.

3. Allow students to make observations over a two-week period.

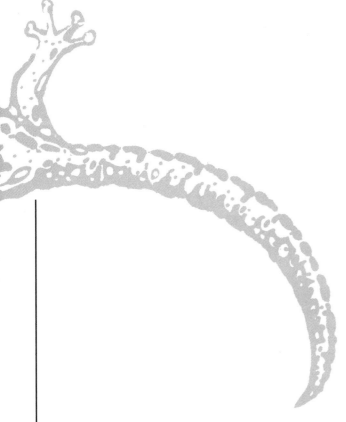

Conclusion:

1. Encourage the class to discuss their observations.

2. Ask students to decide, on the basis of all the investigations, whether their mini-ecosystem is a simple entity or a complex one, and to give reasons for their decision.

STEP 4:
Focusing on an Ocean Animal

Have students form the cooperative learning groups they will work in throughout this unit. Explain that each group will research an ocean animal presented in one of the *Zoobooks* and become an expert on it. Distribute the copies of the relevant *Zoobook* to each group.

This lesson requires students to research an ocean animal presented in one of the *Zoobooks* they choose. Before groups begin their research you might want to review the following research procedures and reading strategy tips with them. Using a copy of one of the eight *Zoobooks*, ask students to

- <u>Skim</u> the pictures and paragraphs to find main topics covered
- <u>Locate</u> main ideas in the text in large type
- <u>Scan</u> the *Zoobook's* captions, diagrams, and illustrations to find details that build the main ideas
- <u>Write</u> unfamiliar words, then find and write their definitions

Note: Refer to the *Teaching Strategies* Supplement for additional ideas on research skills and cooperative learning.

Distribute both pages of Activity Sheet 8 to all students and one additional copy to each group. The additional sheet will become the completed and compiled version for that group. Explain that for Lesson 1, each group's task is to choose an ocean animal from its *Zoobook* and do research that can be entered on the Activity Sheet chart. The completed chart, accompanied by an illustration, will be shared with the class and then displayed on a bulletin board or other display area.

First the whole group can decide on the animal in its *Zoobook* on which it will concentrate. Then partner-teams within the group can research and note data appropriate to one column in the chart. When partners hand in their notes, two group members can transfer the data to the group chart while other members draw illustrations to accompany the chart, prepare new word entries for a glossary, and make notes about what they

7

have learned so far that helps them respond to the question: *"What are the components of an ocean ecosystem?"*

The group can elect two members to present the final chart to the class. Encourage group members to make their own individual copies of the completed chart. Invite the class as a whole to study the display of all the charts to find out which of their questions from Step 1 have been answered and which questions still remain.

STEP 5:
Choosing a Unit Project

Explain that each student will be responsible for creating a unit project that shows the components of an ocean ecosystem. You can allow the projects to be done by individuals, by partners, or by the cooperative learning groups, depending on how you have organized your class. Suggest some examples of forms for the unit projects: an "underwater" travel brochure; an audiotape or videotape; a book; a presentation for younger students in your school. Invite students to brainstorm for other unit project ideas and list them on the chalkboard for their classmates to consider. Follow the general steps under "Unit Projects" in the *Teaching Strategies* Supplement (page 17) to begin this ecosystem project.

ECOCONNECTION ACTIVITY

Throughout the next few weeks, allow students the opportunity to observe and record changes in their aquarium, terrarium, or mini-ecosystem. You might want to set up a class observation log containing a space for date, time, observer, and what was observed. As an alternative, you might have students write their observations and conclusions in their journals or in a form they can place in their portfolios.

CURRICULUM CONNECTIONS

Literature:
Settings by the Sea

Invite interested students to find poems about the ocean to read aloud to small groups or to copy and illustrate for a classroom anthology. Suggest that students get together to compare and contrast the moods of the poems and the word pictures in them. Discuss why the ocean is such a popular topic for writers.

Creative Writing:
Grammar Poems

Student partners can use their *Zoobooks* to find words that describe an ocean animal. To utilize grammar concepts, suggest that the writers find words that are appropriate in this poem frame:

_____:_____,_____,
(name of animal)   (-ing verb)   (-ing verb)

_____,_____:
(adjective)   (adjective)

_____
(noun phrase)

Example: DOLPHIN: leaping, searching, swift, smart:
A mind in the water

Invite partners to read their poem chorally to the class. Then put the poems in a folder on a reading table for students to read independently.

Geography:
Ocean Maps

Distribute copies of an outline map of the world. Ask students to color and label the oceans. They can add labels and a map key to indicate where the *Zoobook* animals live, using the cooperative learning charts from Step 4 as a reference.

Music:
Sea Sounds

Play a tape recording of Claude Debussy's *La Mer* or of "The Shark" from Saint-Saens's *Carnival of the Animals*, or of a whale song, which should be readily available in a nature store or museum store. Discuss the ways in which the composers capture the movement and rhythm of the sea. Invite interested students to work with a partner to compose and tape-record their own sea sounds musically. Suggest that your student composers choose an ocean animal to render musically, or capture in sound the changing moods—from calm to stormy—of the ocean.

Art:
Kinds of Pictures

Invite student partners to study all the *Zoobooks* in this module to find different ways of portraying animals. Examples are panoramic views of many animals in their common setting; closeup illustrations of animals performing specific actions; cross-sections of animals that show their constituent parts; diagrams that show and/or label animals' relationships to factors in their environment. Ask the partners to make their own versions of different kinds of *Zoobooks* portrayals and write captions for each one that tell classmates how to read the pictures to get special information about the animal. Display the students' work in your reading center.

Art/Math:
Geometric Shapes

Draw basic shapes (square, circle, oval, rectangle, triangle) on the chalkboard and challenge interested students to go through all eight *Zoobooks* to find animals to be simply portrayed with these shapes. Have students draw these animals by using these basic shapes to draw the main body part. Students can construct this as a game, drawing the basic shape of the animal on one side of an index card and writing the animal's name on the other side. Then artists can show the drawings to classmates and challenge them to use *Zoobooks* to find the animal and name it.

9

Square

Circle

Oval

Triangle

Rectangle

STUDENT PORTFOLIOS

Portfolios provide a way for students to organize the materials they develop in this unit and to assess their own progress. (See page 9 in the *Teaching Strategies* Supplement.) At the end of this lesson, provide students with materials for their portfolio covers and ask them to begin an Ocean Ecosystems Portfolio. Suggest that enclosures from this lesson might include: (1) questions they hope to answer about the ocean and the animals in it; (2) notes about the ocean ecosystem that will help them respond to the problem: *"What are the components of an ocean ecosystem?"* (3) results of the "Investigating an Ecosystem" activity; (4) the completed chart from their cooperative learning group; (5) plans for their unit project; (6) any materials resulting from the Curriculum Connections activities they have done.

Preparing for the next lesson

Now is a good time for students to begin an Ocean Journal, if they have not done so already. Ask students to write entries that sum up their feelings and insights so far about the ocean and the animals in it. Suggest that students make their Ocean Journals an ongoing part of their Ocean Ecosystems Portfolios.

Students should be selecting a book to read that relates to the ocean. They can include reactions to their selection in their portfolios.

TEACHER'S NOTES AND BACKGROUND INFORMATION

Helpful in setting up seawater aquariums in the classroom

Early on in their study of this module, your students may suggest setting up their own aquariums for marine animals. Because two or three weeks are required for conditioning such aquariums before they can support animal life, you may wish to have students begin setting up their aquariums right away. As students build and monitor their aquariums, they will come to understand the properties of seawater and to appreciate the careful balance that enables marine animals to live in it.

Students can work in groups of five or six to make inexpensive seawater aquariums out of gallon glass jars (available from your cafeteria) and other materials readily available from pet stores or science supply houses. Students will also need copies of the steps (Activity Sheet 1) and of the Monitor Record (Activity Sheet 2). While students prepare for and carry out the steps, share with them the information that follows and the "Working Through..." explanations that give the "why" for steps on the Activity Sheet.

(An alternative to having students set up several aquariums in the classroom is to have the entire class do the activity together instead of in small groups. You might get a local pet supply store or parent to donate the necessary equipment. The aquariums could be set up in your classroom or in the media center/library and be available for several classes. Students could then compare their readings—they should be the same but may differ—and discuss the reasons for similarities or differences. The aquariums could remain in the classroom after the activity is completed to allow additional learning experiences throughout the year.)

Background Information

Composition of Seawater: Seawater everywhere is a constant, complex mixture containing most known chemical elements. Sodium and chloride, an ion, are present in high quantities; elements such as uranium and mercury are only detectable through delicate analytic procedures. Because of this ever-present delicate balance, most oceanic and marine shoreline animals cannot tolerate radical fluctuations in their environment. Estuarian animals can tolerate greater fluctuation, because the amounts of salt dissolved in estuaries naturally vary.

Working Through the Steps on Activity Sheet 1

Three cautions about your materials:

1. **Don't wash** the jars with soap! Soap will hurt marine animals, and no matter how hard one tries, the soap can never be entirely removed. Use baking soda or salt instead.

2. **Never allow metal** to come in contact with the aquarium water. (If you choose a store-bought glass aquarium instead of a jar, be certain there are no metal edges.) Metal rusts quickly, producing chemical compounds toxic to marine animals.

3. **Check the jars** for cracks. Fill the jar with water, place it on newspaper, and let it stand for 24 hours.

11

Step 1: Re: lights and a cool temperature (see "Temperature" in the column to the right) incandescent lights produce heat, while fluorescent lights do not. Re: pets, paints, etc., fumes from volatile substances in paints and markers and ammonia fumes from animal waste products dissolve in the air and get into aquarium water. These substances can kill marine animals.

Step 2: If students are going to collect their own seawater, supply them with plastic pails lined with plastic bags. Because the water near the shore tends to be more polluted, collect the water from as far away from the shore as possible. When the pail is full, close the bag with a twist tie. (One gallon of water weighs about eight pounds, so judge how much students can lift.)

If the seawater is to be made with synthetic salts from a pet store or science supply company, follow the directions on the package. Usually, one-half cup of the salts is dissolved in a gallon of spring water or distilled water. Aerate for 24 hours. *Cautions for students:* Do not use tap water, because it is usually contaminated from copper piping. Do not improvise with table salt. (Remind students that seawater contains many types of salt in a delicate balance.)

Steps 3, 4, and 5: The substrate serves for filtration and aeration.

• **Aeration:** Salt water tends to hold less oxygen than freshwater does. An efficient filtration system allows marine life to breathe and invites oxygen-using bacteria, which break down poisonous waste materials in the tank. (Even so, nitrates may build up; the level of nitrates can be reduced by changing about one-fifth of the water every two weeks.)

• **Filtration:** The filter is part of the system that forces air bubbles into the water. The air-water mixture is lighter than the seawater in the jar, so the mixture rises to the top. As it does so, it forces the rest of the water down through the filter. There, large waste particles are trapped by the filter as the water passes through it.

Caution: If students plan to purchase clams, mussels, barnacles, or sea anemones to add to their aquariums, avoid filtration systems that are "too effective"— that is, that filter all materials from the water. These animals are natural filters and will starve if the filters are too effective.

Step 6: The conditioning period of two to three weeks allows bacterial groups in the gravel to transform animal wastes into nontoxic substances.

Step 7: Students should track their Monitor Records daily. Explain how they can use the thermometer, the hydrometer, and the pH paper to record and adjust three vital components of their aquariums.

• **Temperature:** Most nontropical marine organisms tolerate a temperature range between 40-70 degrees F. Individual tolerance levels differ, and while most can tolerate gradual temperature changes, *the ideal temperature is 52-55 degrees F.* (This is why Step 1, locating the aquarium in a cool place, is vital.) After students check the water temperature with their thermometers, they may wish to cool it. This can be done by briefly placing a zip-lock bag with ice in it in the tank.

• **Salinity/Density:** Density is how much a certain amount of a substance weighs in relation to its volume. (For example, a ball of lead has a high density compared to a ball of cotton.) The hydrometer is used to measure the density of the seawater. Because density increases with salinity, the saltier the water, the higher the hydrometer will float. Because seawater animals require a delicately balanced salinity in their ocean habitat, it is important to monitor the density of the water in the aquariums.

Density is affected by temperature. Point out that the numbers on the hydrometer range from 1.000 to 1.025. On a chart, display the figures in the box below so that students can find the appropriate density of the seawater at the temperature they have noted via their thermometers. Explain that students are to add spring water or distilled water if the hydrometer reading is higher than the number on the chart. Invite students to figure out the pattern, or formula, the chart shows.

55 degrees F	= 1.0245-1.0250
60 degrees F	= 1.0240-1.0245
65 degrees F	= 1.0235-1.0240
70 degrees F	= 1.0230-1.0235
75 degrees F	= 1.0225-1.0230

EXPLORING OCEAN ECOSYSTEMS

- **pH Level:** pH level is the degree of acidity or basicity of the water. (Vinegar and lemon juice are examples of acids. Ammonia and baking soda are examples of bases.) By monitoring the pH level in their aquariums, students get an important clue about what is happening with waste removal. Students can measure pH with a kit of pH paper, available at pet stores.

pH is measured on a scale of 0-14. Water with a pH of 7.0 is neutral. A reading above 7.0 indicates the water is basic; the higher the number, the more basic the water. A reading below 7.0 indicates acidity; the lower the number, the more acidic the water.

The pH of the seawater in the aquariums should range from 7.5 to 8.3. The tank has a tendency to become more acidic as time passes. Gravel acts as a buffer to counteract the increasing acidity and keep the solution in a tolerable range. If a pH of 7.5 or lower is measured, then animal wastes are probably accumulating faster than the natural buffer in the gravel can dissolve. To raise the pH, replace half of the aquarium water with new seawater, or add a little baking soda or a small piece of chalk.

Evaluation

1. After the tanks have been conditioned for two or three weeks, have students generalize the properties of seawater on the basis of their recorded data.

2. Have students compare the properties of seawater with the properties of freshwater.

3. Have students discuss their responses to the following questions: *"What was the most difficult aspect of maintaining your tank?" "Why do you think this was so?"*

13

1

Setting up a Seawater Aquarium

14

MATERIALS YOU NEED:

- ☐ Glass aquarium or widemouthed one-gallon glass jar
- ☐ Substrate: dolomitic limestone or crushed oyster shells
- ☐ Gravel
- ☐ Seawater

- ☐ Under-gravel filter
- ☐ Plastic tubing (for air line)
- ☐ Air pump
- ☐ Kitchen baster
- ☐ A crab or other animal
- ☐ Towel (for cleanup)

- ☐ Thermometer
- ☐ Hydrometer
- ☐ pH paper
- ☐ Frozen fish or clams for food
- ☐ Air Lift Tubes (connect to air line and undergravel filter)

EXPLORING OCEAN ECOSYSTEMS

STEPS:

1. **Find a location** for the aquarium. It should be in a relatively cool place, under fluorescent lights, and away from any other classroom pets (mice, hamsters, etc.) and from paints, markers, etc.

2. **Prepare the seawater** you will use. (Consult with your teacher.)

3. **Rinse the substrate** (limestone or crushed oyster shells) in tap water until the runoff is clear. Then assemble the under-gravel filter (follow the simple instructions provided with the filter or consult with your teacher). Place the under-gravel filter in the bottom of the jar and put the substrate on top of it.

4. **Rinse the gravel** until the runoff is clear. Add the gravel on top of the substrate. Substrate and gravel should be about two inches high in the bottom of the jar.

5. **Place a towel** over the substrate to keep it in place while you carefully pour the seawater into the jar to the desired level. Then remove the towel.

6. **Connect the thin air line tubing** running through the uplift tube on the under-gravel filter to the air pump. Plug in the pump. Bubbles should come out of the tubing.

7. **Use your Monitor Record** to keep a daily log to record the temperature, salinity, and pH in your aquarium for a two-week period.

8. **When you have achieved** the acceptable ranges for pH, density, and temperature, add a small crab or lobster to the jar. Feed the animal small bits of frozen fish or clams. Do not overfeed. Allow it five minutes to eat. Then remove the leftovers with a kitchen baster before they can foul the tank.

9. **Reminders:**

   (a) Scrape algae off the walls of the jar with a straight-edged tool such as a tongue depressor, spoon, bread knife, etc., then remove the algae with a kitchen baster.

   (b) Cloudy water indicates unwanted bacterial growth. It is best to start the tank over again with new seawater.

   (c) If the crab, lobster, or another of your seawater animals become sick, remove it immediately to a "sick bay" jar.

15

Zoobooks®

ACTIVITY SHEET

2

Monitor Record: Seawater Aquarium

Monitor's Name _____

Directions: In column 1, write the dates you make your analysis. In columns 2, 3, and 4, enter the <u>temp</u>erature, <u>salinity</u>/<u>densit</u>y, and p<u>H</u> for each date. Use the last column, 5, for notes about adjustments or observations you make.

1	2	3	4	5
DATE	TEMPERATURE	SALINITY/DENSITY	pH	NOTES

EXPLORING OCEAN ECOSYSTEMS

Setting up a Freshwater Aquarium

MATERIALS YOU NEED:

- ☐ Glass aquarium or widemouthed one-gallon glass jar
- ☐ Substrate: dolomitic limestone or crushed oyster shells
- ☐ Gravel
- ☐ Water
- ☐ Aquarium water conditioner (available at pet stores)
- ☐ Under-gravel filter
- ☐ Plastic tubing (for air line)
- ☐ Air pump
- ☐ Thermometer
- ☐ Kitchen baster
- ☐ Fish or other animal
- ☐ Aquatic plants
- ☐ Fish food
- ☐ pH paper
- ☐ Towel (for cleanup)

17

STEPS:

1. **Find a location** for the aquarium. It should be in a relatively cool place, under fluorescent lights, and away from any other classroom pets (mice, hamsters, etc.) and from paints, markers, etc.

2. **Prepare the freshwater** you will use. Follow the directions on the aquarium water conditioner package. *Note:* water will evaporate from your aquarium. Make sure you add only treated water. Untreated water contains chlorine, which can harm fish.

3. **Rinse the substrate** (limestone or crushed oyster shells) in tap water until the runoff is clear. Then assemble the under-gravel filter (follow the simple instructions provided with the filter or consult with your teacher). Place the under-gravel filter in the bottom of the jar and put the substrate on top of it.

4. **Rinse the gravel** until the runoff is clear. Add the gravel on top of the substrate. Substrate and gravel should be about two inches high in the bottom of the jar.

5. **Place a towel** over the substrate to keep it in place while you carefully pour the water into the jar to its desired level. Then remove the towel.

6. **Connect the thin air line tubing** running through the uplift tube on the under-gravel filter to the air pump. Plug in the pump. Bubbles should come out of the tubing.

7. **Use your Monitor Record** to keep a daily log to record the temperature and pH in your aquarium for a two-week period.

8. **When you have achieved** the acceptable ranges for pH and temperature, add your animal to the jar. Feed the animal small bits of frozen fish or clams. Do not overfeed. Allow it five minutes to eat. Then remove the leftovers with a kitchen baster before they can foul the tank.

9. **Reminders:**

   (a) Scrape algae off the walls of the jar with a straight-edged tool such as a tongue depressor, spoon, bread knife, etc., then remove the algae with a kitchen baster.

   (b) Cloudy water indicates unwanted bacterial growth. It is best to start the tank over again with new water.

   (c) If any of your freshwater animals becomes sick, remove it immediately to a "sick bay" jar.

ACTIVITY SHEET

4

Monitor Record: Freshwater Aquarium

Monitor's Name _____

Directions: In column 1, write the dates you make your analysis. In columns 2 and 3 enter the <u>temperature</u> and <u>pH</u> for each date. Use the last column, 4, for notes about adjustments or observations you make.

	1	2	3	4
	DATE	TEMPERATURE	pH	NOTES
18				

EXPLORING OCEAN ECOSYSTEMS

Zoobooks®
ACTIVITY SHEET
5
BUILDING A TERRARIUM

MATERIALS YOU NEED:

- ☐ Glass aquarium or widemouthed one-gallon glass jar
- ☐ Lid with holes for air
- ☐ Gravel or sand
- ☐ Potting soil
- ☐ Plants
- ☐ Small insects
- ☐ Insect food
- ☐ Small vertebrate: lizard, frog, snake

- ☐ Water bowl
- ☐ Water
- ☐ Sticks
- ☐ Rocks
- ☐ Paper towels
- ☐ Newspapers
- ☐ Optional: heating element needed for lizards and snakes

STEPS:

1. **Clean the aquarium** or jar with warm water and dry with the paper towels.

2. **Cover the work area** with newspaper. Pour the sand or gravel into the bottom of the aquarium to provide drainage. Cover with several inches of potting soil. Moisten the soil with water.

3. **Add the plants** and cover the roots with soil. Add the rocks and twigs to the terrarium.

4. **Fill the water bowl** with water. Add the heating element to give your lizard or snake warmth at night.

5. **Add the insects**, insect food, and other animals to your terrarium. Cover with a lid that allows air to enter the tank.

6. **Add fresh water** and food daily. Clean the terrarium at least once a week.

7. **Observe your terrarium** to see how the living and nonliving things interact.

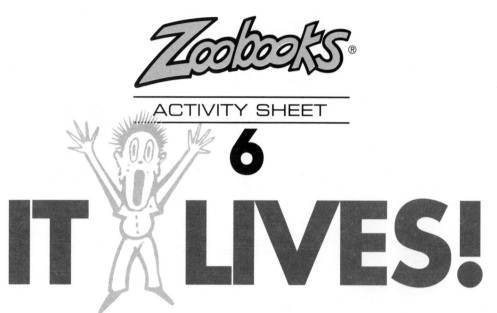

IT LIVES!

1. List all of the living elements in your terrarium. _____

_____

2. List all of the nonliving elements in your terrarium. _____

20 _____

Observation Record
Directions: Observe the living and nonliving parts of your terrarium and record your observations below.

DATE	OBSERVATIONS

Conclusions:

1. In what ways do the living parts interact with the nonliving parts? _____

_____

_____

2. In what ways do the living parts interact with other living parts? _____

_____

_____

3. Is your terrarium a simple or complex system? _____ Why? _____

_____

_____

EXPLORING OCEAN ECOSYSTEMS

ACTIVITY SHEET

7

Observing a Natural Mini-Ecosystem

1. Draw a picture of your mini-ecosystem on a blank piece of paper.

2. List the living components of the mini-ecosystem you are observing. _____

_____

_____

_____

21

3. List the nonliving components of the mini-ecosystem you are observing. _____

_____

_____

_____

4. Observe your mini-ecosystem for five minutes to discover ways the living and nonliving parts interact.

(a) In what ways do the living parts interact with the nonliving parts? _____

_____

_____

(b) In what ways do living parts interact with other living parts? _____

_____

_____

5. Is your mini-ecosystem a simple or complex system? _____ Why? _____

_____

_____

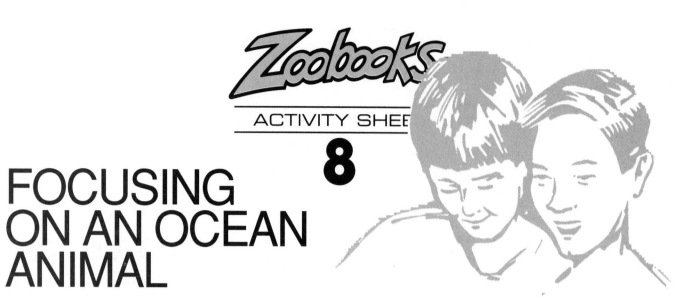

FOCUSING ON AN OCEAN ANIMAL

8

My group's animal is the _____

Things To Find Out	My Predictions
1. Describe fully the animal's appearance. What kind of animal is it (mammal, bird, reptile, etc.)? Describe its size and how it moves.	
2. In what areas of the world's oceans can you find this animal? What is special about the seawater and other geographical and climatic features in these areas?	
3. What are the living and nonliving parts of this animal's ecosystem?	
4. What does the animal eat? How does it get its food? What other ocean animals seek out this animal for their food?	
5. What particular hazards does this animal face as it moves about in its environment?	

22

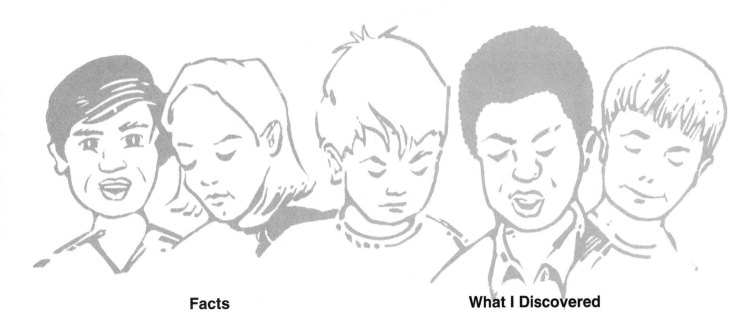

Facts	**What I Discovered**

23

LESSON

2

DIFFERENT HABITATS

The ocean contains a variety of habitats that support living things.

INTRODUCTION

A habitat is the place where an organism normally lives and meets its needs for survival. Students begin by identifying components of their habitat and then transfer this knowledge to understand the habitat needs of ocean animals. After they can identify the components of a habitat, they play the "Habitat Jeopardy Game," making up questions themselves and answering other students' questions about an animal's specific habitat. The lesson concludes by having students depict an animal's habitat and then combine their habitat drawings to show how animals interact in an ecosystem.

OBJECTIVES:

1. To investigate major components of a habitat
2. To collect and organize data about different habitats

YOU NEED:

1. Copies of the eight *Zoobooks* in this module
2. For the science investigation:
   - File cards or slips of paper, 3" x 5"
   - Pencils
   - Butcher paper or chalkboard space
3. Reference materials: general and nature encyclopedias
4. Writing and art materials
5. Activity Sheet 9

LESSON OUTLINE

Before the lesson begins:

1. Duplicate Activity Sheet 9.
2. Collect copies of the *Zoobooks* in the module and the materials needed for the lesson.

During the lesson:

1. Follow the lesson steps to have students
   (a) Fill out Activity Sheet 9 and brainstorm for their understanding of their habitat.
   (b) Define the term HABITAT.
   (c) Create and play the "Habitat Jeopardy Game."

EXPLORING OCEAN ECOSYSTEMS

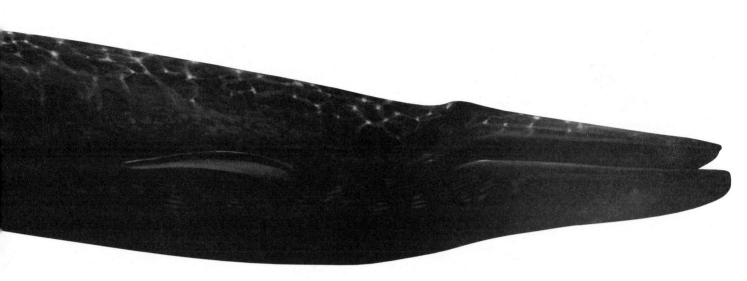

(d) Work in their groups to depict a habitat and then bring the habitats together into an ecosystem.

(e) Continue with their unit projects, Ocean Journals, reading, and portfolios.

(f) Continue to collect articles from newspapers, magazines, and other sources about the world's oceans.

2. Words to add to your **Classroom Glossary:**

Habitat
Population
Space
Shelter

STEP 1:

Brainstorming for Prior Knowledge

Pass out Activity Sheet 9—*My Habitat*. Have students fill it out and discuss where they get their needs for survival. You may wish to discuss the terms "shelter" (where an animal goes for protection, or to be safe) and "space" (the usual part of a habitat where an animal seeks food). Conclude by asking students to compare and contrast depictions of their habitat webs.

STEP 2:

Defining Terms: <u>Habitat</u>

A <u>habitat</u> is the place where an organism normally lives and meets its needs for survival. These needs are food, water, shelter, space, and air. (**Teacher Note:** Not everything needs air to survive. Anaerobic organisms exist without air, but we include air as a necessity because the ocean animals we are discussing all need air to survive.)

Examples of habitats in the ocean ecosystems are kelp beds, tidal areas, tide pools, or the deep ocean. While habitats of different populations overlap in an ecosystem, the parts that make up individual habitats vary from one to another.

Invite members of the cooperative learning groups organized in Lesson 1 to contribute to a Class Habitat chart (similar to the chart on the next page), drawn on the chalkboard, which shows the food, water, shelter, space, and air needs of the different ocean animals the groups are studying in their *Zoobooks*. Ask students to (1) describe or define the various entries (for example, answering the question: *"What is plankton?"*) as you write them into the chart; (2) use a map of the world to point to "spaces" where the animals live. Leave the chart on the board to use in developing vocabulary. To help students understand this, invite students to first read down the columns to describe the habitat of each animal, then compare and contrast the habitats of all the animals.

ANIMALS	RISSO'S DOLPHIN	SEA OTTER	LEMON SHARK
Food	Squid and fish	Shellfish, sea urchins, squid	Fish and squid
Water	From its food	From its food	From its food
Shelter	Open water	Kelp beds, rocks	Open water
Space	Coastal waters	Coastal waters	Coastal waters
Air	From air above water	From air above water	From air in water, through gills

STEP 3:

Investigation: Playing "Habitat Jeopardy"

Estimated time: 2-3 class periods

This game provides an opportunity for students to extend and share their knowledge of ocean animals and their habitats.

Procedure:

1. On oaktag or butcher paper, prepare a "Jeopardy" category-and-scoring chart like the one shown at right. Explain that students will work with a partner to write five or six "answer cards" based on information in a *Zoobook* of their choosing and on what they learned during the brainstorming activity. Partners should develop at least one answer card in each of the categories: animal, food, shelter, and space. Here is an example of an answer card to elicit the question *What is a beluga whale?*:

> This animal is a toothed whale found in coastal water and noted for its beautiful, creamy-white skin. It eats fish, squid, and crabs.

2. Collect the answer cards. The teacher decides on the difficulty level of the answers and accordingly assigns a point value—10, 20, or 30—to them for the Jeopardy Board.

3. Divide the class into teams. Explain that teams will take turns, a team member choosing a category and a point value from anywhere on the board—for example, "Food for 30." The teacher reads an applicable answer card, and the team member gives the question. If the question is the correct one, the team is awarded the points. If the question is incorrect, it is the next team's turn to give the correct question. The next answer card goes to the next team.

4. The teacher can keep score, or appoint a student volunteer to do so. Play can continue until all the answer cards are used, or until one team has achieved a number of points pre-decided by the class.

Conclusion:
Have students summarize what they have learned from this activity about the habitat of an ocean animal not previously studied with their cooperative learning group or answer-card partner.

Animals	Food	Shelter	Space
10	10	10	10
20	20	20	20

SCORES:

Team 1:   Team 2:   Team 3:

ANIMAL
• This animal is a toothed whale found in coastal water and noted for it's beautiful, creamy white skin. It eats fish, squid and crabs.

EXPLORING OCEAN ECOSYSTEMS

STEP 4:

Illustrating Data About a Specific Habitat

Ask students to return to their cooperative learning groups. Invite each group to develop a large picture or illustrated diagram on oaktag or mural paper that shows and labels the components of the habitat of the animal they began studying in Step 4 of Lesson 1. (The components are food, shelter, water, space, and air.) After the individual pictures have been presented to the class, the pictures can be joined and displayed as a mural. First the whole group can discuss the components that they will show. Then individual members can research for pictures and other data needed to accurately depict specific components. After research is completed, students return to the group, share their information, and work together to design and develop their habitat picture.

STEP 5:

Continuing the Unit Projects

Suggest that students brainstorm lists of how they might depict habitats in their unit projects, then collect the materials they will need for these depictions and continue their work on the projects.

ECOCONNECTION ACTIVITY

Ask students to identify the living and nonliving components of the aquarium, terrarium, or mini-ecosystem. Encourage students to brainstorm what other components could be added to this mini-habitat. Encourage students to compare and contrast this human-made environment to a natural ocean ecosystem.

CURRICULUM CONNECTIONS

Social Studies:
Human Habitats

Have students relate how the habitats of their families have changed over the past three generations. How is their habitat different from those of their parents, grandparents, and great-grandparents? You may want to begin this as a class discussion, but then have students portray the different habitats with an oral, written, photographic, or video presentation.

Expository Writing:
From General to Specific

Discuss the construction of many paragraphs in science writing: A first, or topic, sentence makes a general statement. The next sentences give details and examples to support the statement. Invite students to find such paragraphs in their *Zoobooks* and read them aloud to classmates. Then suggest that students use these paragraphs as models to write their own paragraphs about the habitat of the ocean animal they are studying. As a start-up to engender topic sentences, explain that a science paragraph usually answers an important question on a topic. Write the following question on the board and show how to change it into a statement that can be a topic sentence.

Wandering Albatross

• *What are the special characteristics of the penguin's habitat?*

Explain that the statement would be followed by details to show what these characteristics are. After students have gone over their paragraphs with an editing partner, suggest that they put the finished paragraphs in their <u>Ocean Ecosystems Portfolios</u>.

Math:
Writing and Solving Word Problems

Suggest that students make up word problems based on information in one or more of the eight *Zoobooks* in this module.

Storm Petrel

1 *A full-grown petrel weighs about one-half ounce. How much heavier than a petrel is a wandering albatross?*
(See *Seabirds*)

2 *A sea turtle can swim at a speed of up to 15 miles per hour. Find out how fast a penguin and a common dolphin can swim. Then describe the results of a 90-mile long water race between the three animals.*
(See *Seabirds* and *Dolphins* and *Porpoises*)

Explain that the problem-solvers should be able to figure out the answers by consulting the *Zoobooks* named by the writer. You may wish to start with a couple of examples.

Put the finished word problems in a folder in the math center for students to research, discuss, and solve with a partner.

Preparing for the next lesson

Ask each student to continue building his or her <u>Ocean Ecosystems Portfolio</u> with materials developed in this lesson. As a review strategy, suggest that students make a rough draft listing the folder's contents thus far. Explain that the list, revised as the student wishes later on, will eventually become a Table of Contents for the folder.

30

ACTIVITY SHEET

9

MY HABITAT

Complete this web to tell about *your* habitat. It might be a good idea to use a pencil at first, rather than a pen.

31

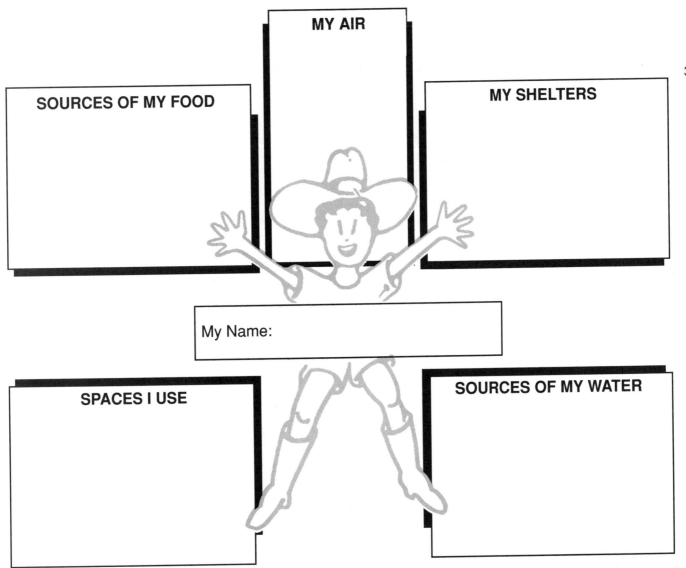

MY AIR

SOURCES OF MY FOOD

MY SHELTERS

My Name:

SPACES I USE

SOURCES OF MY WATER

Zoobooks®

LESSON

3

INTERACTIONS

The living things interact in an ocean environment to meet their needs.

INTRODUCTION

All living things in an ecosystem must share resources for their needs—<u>food</u>, <u>water</u>, <u>shelter</u>, <u>space</u>, and <u>air</u>. It is thought that they must interact and reach a balance of use of those resources for survival. In this lesson, students continue to build their definition and understanding of an ecosystem and the balance of resources its living components must attain to survive. Students investigate these interactions and relationships through a simulation, and by learning about the interactions of a particular ocean animal.

OBJECTIVES:

1. To investigate interactions in an ocean ecosystem
2. To describe the interactions of a particular ocean animal

YOU NEED:

1. Copies of the eight *Zoobooks* in this module
2. For the science investigation:
   - butcher paper and marker
   - large playing area (field or gym)
   - cones or ropes to mark boundaries
3. Writing and art materials

LESSON OUTLINE

Before the lesson begins:

1. Assemble the materials needed.
2. Decide on and secure an area in which to play the "Whale Search Game." It should be in an area where you can have two boundary lines that are at least 25 feet but not more than 25 yards apart.

During the lesson:

1. Follow the lesson steps to have students
   - (a) Brainstorm for prior knowledge of how the food, water, shelter, air, and space support the living things in an ecosystem.
   - (b) Define the term INTERACT.
   - (c) Play the "Whale Search" simulation game and chart how a whale population will peak, decline, and rebuild as its needs are met by its environment.
   - (d) Form cooperative learning groups and write or illustrate a journal entry titled "A Day in the Life of (the group's chosen ocean animal)."
   - (e) Continue with their unit projects, portfolios, reading, and Ocean Journals.
2. Words to add to your **Classroom Glossary:**

   Interact
   Survive
   Simulation

STEP 1:

Brainstorming for Prior Knowledge

On the chalkboard, make columns headed FOOD, AIR, WATER, SHELTER, and SPACE, and, for each of these components, invite students to give examples of the ways these things are provided in their daily life. Discuss whether human life would be sustainable if one of these major components were no longer available, and ask students to explain their responses. Tell students that in this lesson they will investigate how ocean animals also depend upon and seek out these basic necessities.

Food	Air	Water	Shelter	Space

STEP 2:

Defining Terms: Interact

Invite students to identify living and nonliving things that ocean animals encounter as they get food, shelter, and air; discuss spaces, or ocean areas, that the animals use in these pursuits. Suggest that students refer to the habitat mural they created in Step 4 of Lesson 2 to give examples. Then write the following definition on the chalkboard:

Point out that the class has been describing interactions of ocean animals with other things in their environment. Ask if there are any examples of needs the animals can meet without interactions with living or nonliving things. (There are none.) Suggest that students write the definition and make notes of examples to refer to as they build their definitions of an ecosystem.

33

FOOD **SPACE** **SHELTER**

STEP 3:

Investigation: Playing "Whale Search"

Estimated time: 1–2 class periods

This game provides an opportunity for students to understand, through simulation, the interactions of an ocean animal—a whale—as it seeks food, space, and shelter. The game is especially enjoyable to students if they can play it at a brisk pace.

Simulation Pointers:

1. Before the game, discuss what a simulation is and how simulations can help us to understand things we can't directly experience ourselves.

2. Discuss with the class how the game will work.

3. Play the game outside or in a gym.

4. For safety, make sure that students walk during the game.

5. During the game, have the whales stand and the other habitat components sit when tagged.

Procedure:

1. Mark two parallel lines, at least 25 feet but no more than 25 yards apart, on the playground field or gym floor. Prepare a data sheet on butcher paper like the one at the right to record the number of whales "surviving" after each round of the game. (Each round represents one year.)

2. Ask students to count off 1 to 4. The 1's are whales, and stand behind one of the lines. The 2's, 3's, and 4's represent the habitat components of food, space, and shelter, and stand behind the other line.

3. Demonstrate the signals that all players will use: whales looking for food and habitat components representing food will rub their stomachs; similarly, the signal for "space" will be a swimming motion, and the signal for "shelter" will be the player holding his or her nose as if diving deeper into the water.

4. Each round of the game begins with the <u>whales and the habitat components facing away from each other</u>. Each player decides what he or she will represent in that round through the signals you've demonstrated. For example, whales who decide they want space will decide on the

EXPLORING OCEAN ECOSYSTEMS

Whale Search Data Sheet		
Round ("Year")	Whales Surviving	Components Available
1		
2		
3		
4		
5		
6		
7		
8		
9		
10		
11		
12		
13		
14		
15		

of whales surviving, and the component resources available. Then transfer and track on a chart like the one that follows the number of whales that remain after each round, or "year." Players—whales and components—can use a different signal in each round.

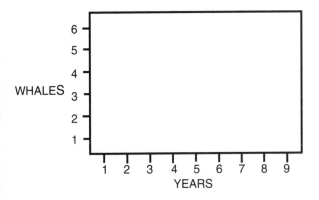

Whale Search Score Chart

Conclusion:

1. Invite students to discuss their feelings and observations as they played this game.

2. Display the completed score chart. Discuss what it shows about a whale population peaking, declining, and rebuilding over the course of the years/game rounds, depending upon the availability of food, shelter, and space.

3. Invite students to answer the following questions: *"What happens to an animal population when there are few resources?" "What happens when resources are abundant?"* Explain.

4. Discuss the relative time that cycles take in nature (as opposed to in a game) and what additional factors come into play (weather, pollution, etc.) in the complex interaction of animals and their resources.

STEP 4:

Describing Interactions

Ask students to return to their cooperative learning groups. Invite each group to write and illustrate a journal entry or picture panel titled "A Day in the Life of (the group's chosen ocean animal)," describing the interactions of the animal with its environment as it meets its needs for

35

swimming motion. Habitat components who want to represent food will decide on the rubbing-the-stomach motion. Caution students that they are not to change their signals during the course of the round.

5. When students are ready, signal them to turn around and make their signals clearly. Habitat components may move around behind their line but may not cross it, while whales move toward them to tag and capture a component that's making the same sign as the whale.

6. If two whales aim for the same component, the whale that captures the component first wins, and takes the component behind the whale line on the playing field. Now the former habitat component is a whale. Explain to students that this represents the whale successfully meeting its needs and successfully reproducing as a result. If a whale fails to find its signaled need, it "dies," and—in this game—moves to the habitat-component team. This represents the dead whale decomposing and eventually becoming a food resource component for other animals.

7. Play 10 to 15 rounds of the game. Record on your data sheet each round or "year," the number

food, shelter, and space. First the whole group can brainstorm a list of important points to cover in the journal entry. Then partners can carry out specific research, writing, and illustrating tasks. Suggest that groups assign two or three members to edit and proofread the entry. After the journal entries have been shared with the class, the class can combine their journal entries and picture panels into one big book.

The journal entry and picture panels become a two-page spread in the book, and all the spreads combine to create a big book you can have at your science center table.

STEP 5:
Continuing the Unit Projects

Remind students to include information about interactions, in written or visual form, in their unit projects.

When this is done, the projects should be in their "final rough draft" form. Students may wish to confer with you or with a partner to discuss their progress on the projects.

ECOCONNECTION ACTIVITY

Have students describe interactions they observe in their aquarium, terrarium, or mini-ecosystem and explain how the animals share resources. They can record these observations in their journals.

CURRICULUM CONNECTIONS

Social Studies:
An Interaction Web

Have students create a diagram of their interactions during one day. Have them place themselves at the middle, and then "connect" themselves to the places they go, the things they do, and the people they interact with. You can expand this activity by having students create a narrative about one or more of these interactions. Suggest that they describe the events that take place, their feelings, what they like or dislike, how they would change it, or other relevant and significant aspects. They can do this in written, oral, video, or art form.

Building Reading Skills:
Using Prefixes

Write the following definition and word list on the chalkboard. Invite students to tell or find the meanings of the words, then say the word with the prefix "inter." Explain how the meaning changes, and use the new word in a sentence.

inter-, prefix: among; between; together; one with the other

action	changeable	city
coastal	cultural	dependent
national	scholastic	state
tidal	twine	

As a follow-up activity, ask students to scan their *Zoobooks* for words that use common prefixes. Have them present these words to the group in a sentence context, and challenge classmates to define the words.

Preparing for the next lesson

Ask students to continue building their Ocean Ecosystems Portfolios with materials developed in this lesson and to update their Table of Contents list. This might be a good time to confer with students about whether or not they feel their portfolios are helping them to reach their stated learning goals. (A sample conference sheet is included in your *Teaching Strategies* Supplement on page 13.) As a preview strategy for the next lesson, "The Food Web," suggest that students look over the materials in their folders to note and remember facts about the food needs of ocean animals.

LESSON

4

THE FOOD WEB

The living things form a food web through which energy flows throughout the ocean ecosystems.

INTRODUCTION

All living things need energy to survive. Plants are the primary energy producers in all ecosystems. They obtain their energy from the sun and pass it along to others in the ecosystem through a series of steps of eating and being eaten. This process is known as a food chain. Within ecosystems, food chains overlap and become interlinked, forming a food web. This lesson contains a simulation in which students become ocean plants and animals and pass food (in the form of peanuts) to others in the food web.

OBJECTIVES:

1. To investigate how the energy flows through a food web within ocean ecosystems
2. To identify the relationship between different plants and animals in the ocean's food web

YOU NEED:

1. Copies of the eight *Zoobooks* in this module

2. For "Defining Terms" and the science investigation:
   - Copies of Activity Sheets 10 and 11
   - Peanuts in shell, 4 to 5 pounds depending on class size
   - Teacher-made signs for students to wear around their necks:
     1 each: Sun, Human, Orca Whale, Shark, Sea Turtle, Blue Whale; **5** Fish; **9** Krill; **12** Algae
   - Chart, marker for recording
   - Large game area, outside or in gym
3. Reference materials
4. Writing and art materials

LESSON OUTLINE

Before the lesson begins:

1. Make the signs to be worn by students, described in 2 above.
2. Select an appropriate area, either in a gym or outside, where students can play "The Web Game" simulation.
3. Duplicate Activity Sheets 10 and 11, which students will use during the lesson.

During the lesson:

1. Follow the lesson steps to have students
   (a) Brainstorm for prior knowledge. Show students that everything they eat originates in the form of energy from the sun.
   (b) Define the term FOOD WEB.
   (c) Play "The Web Game."
   (d) Understand how food energy flows "up" through a food chain and how delicate the balance of food and food consumers is in such a web.
   (e) Depict the food web of the specific ocean animal their group is studying.
   (f) Complete their unit projects.

39

2. Words to add to your **Classroom Glossary:**

Food chain
Food web
Primary consumer
Secondary consumer
Decomposer
Scavenger
Carnivore
Herbivore
Omnivore

STEP 1:
Brainstorming for Prior Knowledge

Tell students that you believe they all ate the same thing yesterday. After any protests, explain that they all had sunshine, because all food can be traced back to the sun. Use examples from sandwich ingredients. For example, the peanuts in peanut butter come from a plant that gets its energy from the sun; cheese comes from milk, which comes from a cow, which eats grass, which

gets its energy from the sun. Elicit the names of other foods and discuss where they came from and where each type gets its energy (plants, from the sun; animals, from other animals or from plants). All links will eventually go back to the sun. Ask students to predict whether this will hold true for the ocean ecosystems, too. Then invite members of the cooperative learning groups to develop questions they'd like answered about the group's ocean animal and its place in the ocean's food web.

STEP 2:
Defining Terms: <u>Food Web</u>

Distribute Activity Sheet 10, which is a graphic representation of the generalized definition of a food web. Review the terms "food chain" and "food web" with students, and then ask them to define <u>food web</u> on the Activity Sheet. Help students work toward their definitions by discussing the following ideas:

- All living things depend on the sun for energy, either directly (producers) or indirectly (consumers).

Zoobooks®

- Producers, usually plants, use the sun's energy to create their own food.
- Consumers, usually animals, use plants or other consumers as an energy source. <u>Primary consumers</u> (herbivores) eat plants. <u>Secondary consumers</u> (carnivores, insectivores, omnivores) eat either animals that are primary consumers or other secondary consumers.
- Decomposers and scavengers, e.g., bacteria, snails, and worms, break down plant and animal matter, making gases, water, and nutrients that are then re-used by other living things.

Encourage students to compare and contrast the food sources, functions, and contributions of producers, consumers, and decomposers in another ecosystem they are familiar with. Then invite students to predict which roles (producer, consumer, decomposer) are played by the ocean animals they are studying. Use students' responses to create several chalkboard food webs with the class.

STEP 3:

Investigation: Playing "The Web Game"

Estimated time: 1 class period

This game provides an opportunity for students to see how energy flows throughout an ocean ecosystem. It should be played in a large area outside or in a gym.

Procedure:

1. Distribute the signs. (If you have fewer or more than 32 students in your class, keep the roles of 1 sun and 1 human, but make the other roles proportionate by dropping out a turtle or a shark. You need more students at the bottom of the food pyramid (producers or algae) and fewer students at the top (secondary consumers, which are all the players <u>but</u> algae and krill).

2. The student playing the "sun" is the keeper of energy (the peanuts), and gives five peanuts at a time to each student playing "algae." Algae are the only players who can get energy in this way, and they may go to the sun anytime to "fuel up."

However, after each fuel-up the algae must move at least 10-15 yards away from the sun. (Instruct students not to eat the peanuts until after the game is over!)

3. Distribute signs to the other players and as you explain the following rules, tell students to write what foods they can eat on the backs of their signs so they won't forget.

- Krill can tag only algae.
- Sea turtles can tag krill or algae.
- Blue whales can tag krill or algae.
- Fish can tag only krill.
- Orca whales can tag only fish.
- Sharks can tag only fish.
- Humans can tag any player.
- Tagged players must give up two peanuts to their taggers.

4. Designate the playing-field boundaries and decide on the time limit of the game. Suggested: five to eight minutes. After algae fuel up with their energy (peanuts) the tagging begins.

5. After "Time!" is called, ask each group (algae, krill, fish, whales, humans, sharks, and turtles) to get together and count and record its number of peanuts. Algae, as a group, will probably have the largest number, krill the next largest number, etc.

Conclusion:

1. Discuss the outcome of "The Web Game." If the proportions are different from the ones suggested in 5 above, discuss why this happened and if a similar series of events could happen in the ocean ecosystems.

2. Suggest that students use Activity Sheet 11 to depict the ocean food web they simulated in the game.

STEP 4:

Focusing on One Animal's Place in the Food Web

Ask students to return to their cooperative learning groups. Suggest that each group develop a complete food web which highlights the position of the group's *Zoobook* animal within it. Groups can present the information to the class as a picture strip, chart, human web, play, or news report. First

40

the whole group can decide on the components of the food web and how to present the information. Then individual members can research one link in the web to determine its role in the energy exchange in the ocean ecosystem. When research is complete, students can return to the group, share their data, and prepare the class presentation.

STEP 5:
Finalizing the Unit Projects

Remind students to include food-web information in their unit projects. Suggest that as they complete their projects, students check to make sure all the components of the ocean ecosystem are accurately portrayed.

ECOCONNECTION ACTIVTY

Is there a food chain or a food web in the aquarium or terrarium? Have students observe their aquarium, terrarium, or mini-ecosystem and describe what they see. They can draw or discuss their observations. Let them suggest other animals they might add to the aquarium. How would this affect the existing food chain(s) and food web? If students are observing a mini-ecosystem in their city, have them describe its food chain or food web.

CURRICULUM CONNECTIONS

Health:
Personal Food Chain

Invite students to list what they ate during a recent meal. Then have them create a food chain of all the foods they ate. They can depict the chain using words, pictures, or diagrams. After they've completed this activity, ask them how they think their food choices have affected their own ecosystem.

Literature:
People on Their Own

Discuss books, stories, literary excerpts, movies, and TV dramas the class has read or seen about people who must suddenly find their own food in wilderness or hardship situations. Examples are in Daniel Defoe's *Robinson Crusoe*, Scott O'Dell's *Island of the Blue Dolphins*, and Jean Craighead George's *Julie of the Wolves*. Invite students to determine the changing or static role of the character in the food web, and the character's new relationship to the ecosystem.

As a follow-up, suggest that students imagine themselves in similar situations and write journal entries to describe how they would get food in a wilderness ecosystem.

Creative Writing:
Animal Adventures

Invite students to write adventure stories from the point of view of an ocean animal seeking and being sought in the food web. Example: A tuna finds and feasts from a school of herring, then narrowly escapes a killer whale and a fishing-boat net. Encourage students to combine accuracy about the ocean ecosystem with imaginative details and vivid descriptive phrases. Students can present their written stories in a <u>Class Ocean Autobiographies folder</u>, use them as the basis for tell-aloud tales to share with younger children in school or at home, or prepare them as picture panels to display around the room.

42

Unit Wind-Up and Assessment

1. The lesson assessment begun in Lesson 1 may now be completed by having students fill out the third section, "What I've discovered about the ocean."

2. Ask small groups of students to review what they have learned by responding to the question posed in Lesson 1: "What are the components of an ocean ecosystem?" Bring the class together to discuss the groups' responses and combine them in a response all students agree to. Students should be able to use the class response to develop a list of what an ocean ecosystem always has, what it sometimes has, and what it never has. Invite students to discuss another ecosystem with which they are familiar and compare and contrast it with the ocean ecosystem to respond to the problem: "What is an ecosystem?"

3. Schedule presentations of the unit projects. Use the criteria you have developed with the class beforehand for students to assess their own and others' unit projects.

4. Ask students to organize their <u>Ocean Ecosystems Portfolios</u>. Allow time for them to complete, revise, or add to the materials, which should include the results of investigations, Ocean Journals, and glossaries. Ask each student to write an evaluation of his or her portfolio to tell what it shows about ideas learned, questions answered, and remaining questions about the ocean that the student may wish to pursue.

10
THE
FOOD WEB

Discuss food webs with your classmates. Then complete the definition below in your own words.

A food web is _____

_____

_____

_____

_____

43

ENERGY PROVIDED BY THE SUN

SECONDARY CONSUMERS

ENERGY

PRIMARY CONSUMER

Shrimp   Krill

ENERGY

PRODUCER
Algae

Plants   Plankton

Waste products, dead producers and dead consumers are acted on by decomposers and scavengers.

WASTE
PRODUCTS

TO ENVIRONMENT

ACTIVITY SHEET

11
CREATING AN OCEAN FOOD WEB

Draw a food web for an ocean animal below. Get ideas by referring to your *Zoobooks*.

44

UNIT 2

Animal Adaptations

Unit Concept:

OCEAN ANIMALS HAVE STRUCTURAL AND BEHAVIORAL ADAPTATIONS THAT ENABLE THEM TO MEET THEIR NEEDS.

- *They have adaptations for obtaining food and oxygen.*

- *They have adaptations to help themselves and their young survive in salt water.*

- *They have adaptations to protect themselves from predators.*

LESSON

1

INTRODUCING ADAPTATIONS

Ocean animals have adaptations for obtaining food and oxygen.

INTRODUCTION

Students begin this lesson by reviewing how ocean animals meet their survival needs. Next, students look at a variety of *Zoobooks* photographs showing structural and behavioral adaptations. Students are guided to create a class definition of the word "adaptation." Next, students explore adaptations in four stations. At Station 1, students tape their thumb to their hand and compare how well they perform various tasks with taped and untaped thumbs. At Station 2, students simulate a baleen whale eating food by using four different tools to collect pepper floating on water. At Station 3, students apply their knowledge of adaptations by creating a bird beak and then discovering which type of food their bird beak can capture most easily. At Station 4, students smell different substances mixed with water to compare their sense of smell to a shark's. Next, students work in groups to create adaptation cards they will use to play the "Memory Game" at the conclusion of this unit. Finally, students begin to work on unit projects.

OBJECTIVES:

1. To investigate specific structural adaptations of ocean animals that enable them to survive in their habitats
2. To relate structure to specific behaviors

YOU NEED:

1. Copies of the eight *Zoobooks* in this module
2. For the science investigation, see the lists of materials for each station
3. Copies of Activity Sheets 12a-12d
4. For the cooperative learning activity, unlined 3" x 5" index cards
5. Reference materials
6. Writing and art materials

LESSON OUTLINE

Before the lesson begins:

1. Duplicate Activity Sheets 12a-112d (one set for each student).
2. Obtain materials for the stations and set up the stations.
3. Gather the 3" x 5" index cards, *Zoobooks*, and other reference materials for the lesson.

During the lesson:

1. Follow the lesson steps to
    (a) Discuss how ocean animals meet their needs in different ways.
    (b) Define the term ADAPTATION.

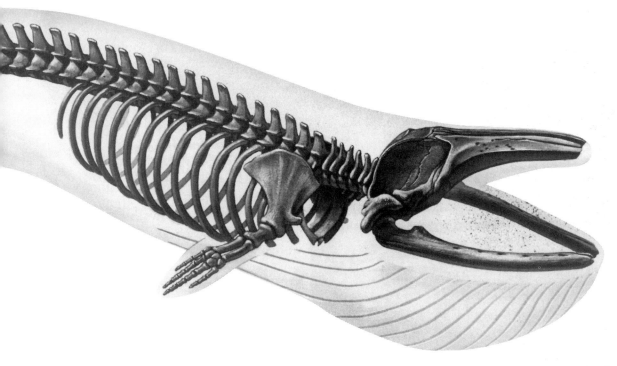

(c) Explain each station and the accompanying Activity Sheet to students.

(d) Monitor students' progress at stations and provide additional help or materials when needed.

(e) Discuss students' experiences at the stations.

(f) Have students form cooperative groups to create picture cards for the Memory Game.

(g) Guide student groups to select and begin a unit project. (**Note:** As you discuss ideas for the unit projects with students, develop criteria with them to evaluate those projects. Refer to page 17 in the *Teaching Strategies* Supplement for ideas on how to do this.)

(h) Have students start an Ocean Animal Adaptations Portfolio.

2. Words to add to your **Classroom Glossary**:

Adaptation
Extinction

STEP 1:

Brainstorming for Prior Knowledge

Review with students the basic components of an ocean habitat (shelter, space, food, water, and air). Discuss how all ocean animals must fill these needs, but do so in different ways. Invite students

to apply this concept to specific animals they've already studied. Explain that in this unit students will investigate another concept that applies to all ocean animals.

47

STEP 2:

Defining Terms: Adaptation

Adaptations are structures or behaviors that allow an animal to meet its needs in the environment. Useful adaptations evolve over long periods of time, because animals with more useful adaptations are more likely to survive and reproduce offspring with the same adaptation. **Teacher Note:** Living organisms inherit physical structures (beak shape) as well as some behaviors (nest building) from their parents. The "blueprints" for inherited characteristics are contained in the genes (DNA) found in cells. An organism with genes that produce features which help it meet its needs in the environment has a greater chance of surviving to adulthood and passing on its genes to its offspring.

When an environment changes, an organism must migrate (move to a more suitable environment) and adapt (change its behavior or physical characteristics to adjust to its new environment), or it will die. Extinction is a natural process which may occur when a species is unable to adapt to meet its survival needs in a changing environment.

To help students understand what is meant by "structural adaptation," have students look at the picture in the *Sea Otters Zoobook* to find physical

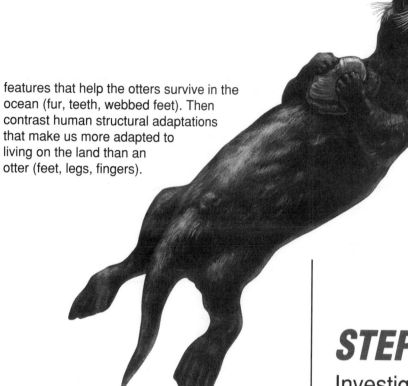

features that help the otters survive in the ocean (fur, teeth, webbed feet). Then contrast human structural adaptations that make us more adapted to living on the land than an otter (feet, legs, fingers).

Ask students if they can name any behaviors that a sea otter or another ocean animal has which enable it to survive in the ocean. Direct students' attention to *Zoobooks* drawings of sea otters using a rock to crack open a shell. Explain that this is a behavior which helps the animal get food. Have students look through the *Zoobooks* to find other examples of adaptive behaviors. Encourage students to identify behavioral adaptations humans have that help us survive. You may want students to start (or continue) an Ocean Journal. Various writing activities throughout the unit can be done in the journal. Invite students to list questions in their journals that they'd like answered about the adaptations of other ocean animals. Compile a class list to keep on display. Have students check off the questions they answer in the course of this unit.

A PROBLEM TO SOLVE: Write the following question on poster paper for display: *"How do structural and behavioral adaptations help ocean animals survive?"* Explain that as students work through this unit they will gather material that will help them solve this problem. A related problem they might solve to reach a generalization is: *"How do structural and behavioral adaptations help any living thing survive?"* Suggest that students begin their solutions by writing down the definition the class has arrived at for adaptation.

STEP 3:
Investigating Adaptations

> Estimated time: 2 class periods

In this activity, each student works in turn at four different stations to investigate different structural adaptations and their purposes. Students use Station Record Sheets (Activity Sheets 12a-12d) to record their findings, answer questions, and draw conclusions.

TIME CONSIDERATION:

These activities were designed to allow about 20 minutes per station. Stations 1, 2, and 4 require less time than Station 3 (building a bird beak). Here are several ways you can organize the stations to adapt to the time constraints:

- Set up two or three sets of materials at each station so you can have smaller groups of students at each of these stations. Students can then rotate to an open station at their own pace.

- Start the whole class at Station 3. Once they understand what to do, have small groups move on to Stations 1, 2, and 4 while students work at their own pace at Station 3.

- Set the stations up as week-long centers in your room. At designated times, or when students have completed other work, allow them to work at the stations.

- Designate a conclusion area. After students finish an activity, they go to the conclusion area to write, leaving the stations open for others to complete the activities.

EXPLORING OCEAN ECOSYSTEMS

GENERAL PROCEDURE:

1. Set up the stations ahead of time. The descriptions that follow include the materials and procedure for each station.

2. Divide the class into four groups and distribute the Station Record Sheets. Each group conducts the activity at a different station, fills out the Record Sheet for that investigation, and then moves on to the next station.

STATION 1

PROBLEM: How do adaptations enable organisms to meet their needs?

Background Information: Humans have opposable thumbs (thumbs opposite their fingers), allowing them a greater range of grasping behaviors than animals without opposable thumbs. Example: Humans can use and manipulate tools because of their thumbs.

Materials Needed: masking tape, five pennies, paper, pencils, eight-inch pieces of string, jars with lids

Procedure:

1. Students wrap tape around one hand to immobilize their thumb and then try the following tasks: print their name, tie the string into a bow, remove a jar lid, and pick up pennies one at a time. They record their experiences on Activity Sheet 12a (Station 1 Record Sheet).

2. Students carry out the same activities without an immobilized thumb and record their experiences.

3. Students answer the questions on the Station 1 Record Sheet and draw the conclusion that thumbs are a beneficial adaptation for humans. Thumbs help people do many fine motor activities necessary for daily life.

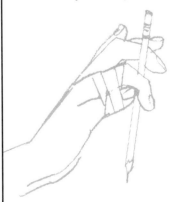

STATION 2

PROBLEM: How does baleen enable baleen whales to get food?

Background Information: Two rows of baleen hang like dense curtains of coarse hair from the humpback whale's upper jaw. The baleen enables the whale to get the huge amounts of algae, plankton, krill, and small fish it needs to sustain itself. The whale scoops up food-rich seawater and strains the water through the baleen, catching the food and pressing out the excess water with its tongue.

Materials Needed: a shallow pan filled with water; 1/2 teaspoon of finely ground black pepper; two or three combs with varying degrees of fineness in their teeth; a small, fine bristle brush; *Whales Zoobooks* opened to show baleen; towels to wipe up spills

Procedure:

1. Sprinkle the pepper into the water. The tiny specks of pepper represent the whale's food.

2. Encourage students to predict which of the available implements will be the best at catching the "food."

3. Invite students to catch the "food" using their fingers and then using each of the implements provided at the station. Have students record their results on Activity Sheet 12b (Station 2).

4. Students should answer the questions on their Station Record Sheets and draw the conclusion that many very fine particles can be caught with a fine, brush-like structure, like baleen. The whale's adaptation allows it to find and consume food in its habitat.

STATION 3

PROBLEM: How do birds' beaks enable them to catch their food?

Background Information: Seabirds have beaks that are adapted to catching particular kinds of food. Some birds are specialists: The structure of their beaks enables them to catch just one kind of food. Other birds are generalists: They have beaks that allow them to catch many different kinds of food.

Materials Needed: *Seabirds* and *Penguins Zoobooks*; materials to construct beaks: clothespins, construction paper, pipe cleaners, toothpicks, scissors, spoons of various

49

sizes, popsicle sticks, brads, paper clips, glue, tape, etc.; materials to represent bird food: marbles, raisins, styrofoam pieces, macaroni in various shapes, small crackers, etc.; small cups to represent stomachs

Procedure:

1. Students choose a bird from the *Zoobooks*. They closely examine the bird's beak and determine what it eats and how it gets its food.

2. Students use the materials to make a facsimile of their bird's beak. Then they simulate use of the beak by using it to pick up the different kinds of "food." Have students put the food they successfully catch with the beak into the paper cup, then tabulate the results on their Station 3 Record Sheets.

3. Ask students to share the results of their investigation with their group and demonstrate the use of the beak. The group can then decide which birds are best adapted to capturing each type of food.

STATION 4

PROBLEM: How can a shark's sense of smell help it detect prey in the ocean?

Background Information: Sharks have several senses to help them detect prey. A shark probably uses its well-developed sense of hearing to locate its prey up to 3,000 feet away. Then the shark uses its keen sense of sight or smell to hone in on the prey. Some sharks can smell one part of blood dissolved in 100 million parts of water.

Others have small holes on their faces that can detect electrical impulses from prey.

Materials Needed: *Sharks Zoobook;* seven small, similarly sized jars (such as baby food jars) labeled 1 to 7; water; eyedropper; six liquids: banana extract, mint extract, lemon juice, vinegar, vanilla, bleach (other available liquids can be substituted)

Procedure:

1. Fill the jars with water. Add two drops of each liquid to a different jar. Make a key identifying the contents of each jar. One jar should have only water.

2. Students take turns smelling the contents of each jar. They use their Station 4 Record Sheets to record what they smelled and whether or not the odor is something to eat. Caution students that they are NOT to taste any of the liquids.

3. Have students compare their guesses with their group, and then answer the questions on their Station 4 Record Sheet.

4. After all of the groups have completed this station, reveal the substances in each jar. Discuss with students which sense they use most often.

CONCLUSION:

1. Encourage students to summarize what they learned about the adaptations at each of the stations.

2. Invite students to predict the answers to the following questions about adaptations and why they are beneficial to the animals. After they have completed their predictions, individuals, pairs, or small groups can look up the answers in the appropriate *Zoobooks.*

   (a) Why do sea otters take such good care of their fur?

   (b) Why do sharks keep swimming in an upward direction, but other fish don't?

   (c) Why do sharks have so many fast-growing teeth?

   (d) Both sea lions and true seals swim, but each has a different adaptation to get around. Compare these two adaptations.

   (e) Why do walruses and other pinnipeds have layers of blubber?

   (f) What adaptation do pinnipeds have to keep water out of their noses?

50

STEP 4:

Focusing on Adaptations

Have students form the cooperative learning groups they will work in throughout the unit. Explain that each group will be responsible for making a deck of picture cards to be used in the Memory Game at the conclusion of the unit. Group members will make several pairs of cards illustrating adaptations of ocean animals. One card in each pair will show a behavior of an animal—for example, a seal swimming. The other card in the pair will be a closeup showing the structure that makes the behavior possible, such as the seal's short, stiff flipper.

Students can perform a variety of roles within each group. The whole group brainstorms adaptations to illustrate, with one student acting as recorder to keep a list of all completed cards and related research. Another student can be the researcher (to find and verify facts); another two students can be illustrators (to draw, create, or locate illustrations for the cards). The groups might also be organized into partner-teams, with each pair responsible for creating certain cards. Work on the deck continues throughout the unit. Advise students to elect one group member to store the cards until they're needed for the Memory Game.

STEP 5:

Choosing a Unit Project

Explain that each student will be responsible for a unit project that shows the structural and behavioral adaptations of animals. These projects can be done by individuals, by partners, or by cooperative learning groups. Suggest some examples of forms for the unit project: mobiles showing different adaptations of one type of ocean animal (the three-dimensional objects on the mobile can be made out of many things, such as papier-mâché, found objects, or wire sculpture); or picture charts that compare and contrast important behaviors, such as getting food, protecting young, moving around, and communicating. Invite students to brainstorm for other project ideas and list them on the chalkboard for their classmates to consider. Follow the general steps in the *Teaching Strategies* Supplement under "Unit Projects" (page 17).

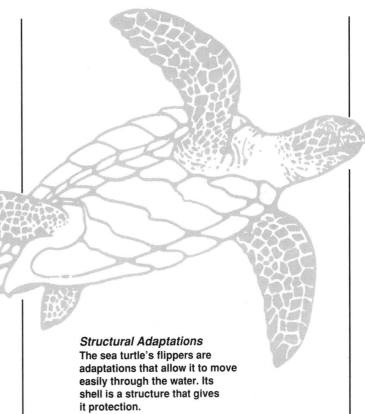

Structural Adaptations
The sea turtle's flippers are adaptations that allow it to move easily through the water. Its shell is a structure that gives it protection.

51

ECOCONNECTION ACTIVITY

As a whole class or in small groups, have students observe the living things in the aquarium, terrarium, or mini-ecosystem. Discuss the structural and behavioral adaptations that enable these organisms to meet their needs.

CURRICULUM CONNECTIONS

Art:
Japanese Fish Prints

Gyotaku is a Japanese print technique that uses whole fish to make prints. Your students can adapt the procedure using seashells, seaweed, or fish bones and fish tails (from your local market). If students want to use a whole fish, try a porgy, but warn students about—or cut off—the sharp top fin. Students will also need tempera paint or water-based linoleum block printing ink, brushes, large sheets of white construction paper, and newspapers to cover their work surface.

Procedure:

1. Allow students the opportunity to look at and feel the object they've chosen. Discuss how the organism's structure helps it meet its needs. Encourage students to infer what types of behaviors the organism uses to meet its needs.

2. Lay the shell, fish, seaweed, or other object on the newspaper and paint the top of it.

3. Lay the construction paper on top and carefully and evenly press it over the painted object or fish, making sure not to move the object or to slide the paper. For some objects, like pointy seashells, you might suggest students stamp the shell onto the paper to create a pattern.

4. Lift the paper off carefully and lay the print flat to dry. If they wish, students can use black markers or paint to highlight features of their prints. Display the prints around the room for a class Ocean Art Gallery.

Here's another challenging use of the prints: Make a paper "pillow" by using yarn to stitch together the print and a piece of heavy paper of the same size. For pillow stuffing, use crumpled sheets of newspaper.

52

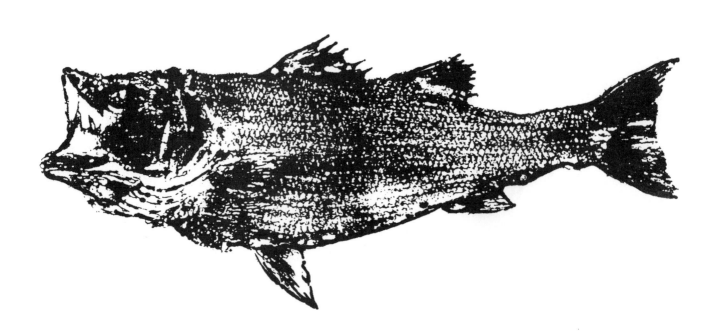

Creative Writing:
Science Fiction

Invite each student to become a science fiction writer—a writer who relies on science as the basis for stories. Then have each student choose a planet and research (or review) its environment. Suggest students list the important components of that environment, such as light, gravity, temperature, air, landform, and water. Once these components are determined, have students design a creature who is well adapted to its specific environment. For instance, if the planet is dark, the creature might have many huge eyes or feelers. Tell students to write a description and create an illustration of their creature. Invite them to share their alien environment and creature with the class. Class members might suggest other ways living things might adapt to that environment. Students can then use these details to write a story about the creature they've created, such as what happens when humans encounter it for the first time, or about what daily life is like on its planet.

Values:
Sensitivity to Human Differences

Develop a sensitivity in students about the problems a disability can create for people in our society and the adaptations both people and society must make. Invite students to carry out a series of "disability" simulations. You may want to avoid simulations that relate to the disabilities of students in your class. Simulations might include a "trust walk" (a blindfolded partner is led around for about five minutes); wearing tight socks over hands while trying to do daily dressing functions; getting around in a wheelchair or on crutches; a spelling test in which words have certain consonants missing and are said too softly; or reading reversed writing.

Simulations like these show how frustrating it is to need to concentrate on simple tasks that other people take for granted. After students attempt these activities, have them write about how they felt while doing them. Discuss the differences between a disability (an inability or diminished capacity to do something in a specific way) and a handicap (a disadvantage imposed on or by the individual that restricts achievement but may

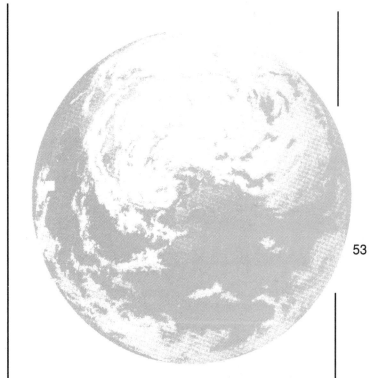

53

or may not be caused by a disability). For instance, being blind is a disability, but it is not a handicap (a restriction) in many situations. Many modern devices, such as braille and talking computers, allow disabled people to adapt to difficult situations in which they would have been handicapped before. Brainstorm for examples of when a disability may not be a handicap, as when a blind person works in a photographic darkroom or plays music; for examples of when disabilities are handicaps, as when a blind person uses an elevator alone; and for devices that can end the handicap, such as having braille on elevator buttons. Brainstorm other ways people have sometimes turned a disability into a handicap, such as by building doorways that are too narrow for wheelchairs. Finally, have students apply this sensitivity by examining how their school or community can be made more accessible to disabled people.

Health:
Maintaining a Healthy Body

Pose the problem: *"How can people maintain a healthy body in today's changing environment?"* Brainstorm with the class what is meant by "a healthy body." Have individuals or teams of students investigate modern risks to good health (examples: smoking, poor diet, and high stress). Have students identify healthy behaviors and risky behaviors. For example, exercising regularly is a healthy behavior and smoking is a risky behavior. Have students create a Warning or Good Health poster and an oral report and present them to an audience of their peers or to younger students. Display the posters throughout the school.

As a final activity, compare humans, who can control many risk factors, to domestic and wild animals, which have less control over risk factors. Brainstorm ways people can control the risk factors for both pets and wild animals, such as controlling pollution or a pet's diet.

STUDENT PORTFOLIOS

Invite students to begin a new portfolio called Ocean Animal Adaptations. Suggest they include in these portfolios: (1) their Ocean Journal, including the questions they would like answered about the adaptations of ocean animals; (2) their Station Record Sheets; (3) their answers to the questions asked about beneficial adaptations of specific ocean animals; (4) their plans for their unit project; (5) any materials they are working on or have completed from the Curriculum Connections. Suggest that their portfolio cover illustrate the adaptations of one or more ocean animals. Encourage them to create a Table of Contents.

Preparing for the next lesson

Invite students to pantomime short scenes showing an ocean animal using a beneficial structural adaptation. Ask the class to identify the structure and the behavior. As a follow-up, suggest students brainstorm all the behaviors that could come from this one structural adaptation, such as a strong flipper being used in swimming and for moving around on land. Remind students to safeguard their Memory Game cards for later use.

ACTIVITY SHEET

12a

STATION RECORD SHEET

STATION 1

Problem: How do adaptations help an organism meet its needs?

Procedure: (1) Tape your thumb to your hand so you cannot move it. Then do each of the following tasks and record your findings on the chart.
(2) Repeat the task without your thumb taped and record your findings on the chart.

TASK	With thumb taped: Name specific difficulties	With thumb free: How is the task easier?
1. Print your name.		
2. Tie a bow.		
3. Comb your hair.		
4. Pick up one penny at a time.		

55

Conclusion:
Is the thumb a useful adaptation? ❑ Yes   ❑ No   If so, tell how:_____

_____

_____

Challenge: Humans have opposable thumbs. To find out what an opposable thumb is, do the tasks above with your thumb free, but do not touch your thumb to your fingers or hold things between them. Then work with a classmate to write a definition of opposable thumb.

_____

_____

Choose an ocean animal and name one of the adaptations it has—either physical or behavioral—that enables it to survive in its environment. Explain. _____

_____

_____

12b

STATION RECORD SHEET
STATION 2

Problem: How does baleen enable baleen whales to get their food?

Procedure: (1) Read about "baleen whales" in the *Whales Zoobook.* (2) Predict which implement at this station will be the best way to "catch" the pepper that is floating on the water.

_____

(3) Try to catch the pepper by using each implement. Record your results on the chart below by ranking each implement 1 to 4, with 1 for the least successful in picking up small specks and 4 for the most successful.

RANK	Fingers	Brush	Wide-toothed comb	Fine-toothed comb

Conclusion:

1. Which implement best duplicates a whale's baleen? _____

Why? _____

_____

_____

2. Why do baleen whales have baleen instead of large, sharp teeth?_____

_____

_____

Challenge: Many kinds of whales and dolphins eat large fish. What structural adaptations enable them to catch and eat these fish? Find the answers by studying your *Zoobooks.* Write the answers and share them with your classmates.

_____

_____

_____

_____

_____

EXPLORING OCEAN ECOSYSTEMS

ACTIVITY SHEET

12c

STATION RECORD SHEET
STATION 3

Problem: How do birds' beaks enable them to catch their food?
Procedure: (1) Fill out parts 1 and 2 below using information you find in the *Seabirds* and *Penguins Zoobooks.* (2) Use this information to build a model of your bird's beak. Record the materials you use. (3) Use the beak for one minute to pick up different types of "food" and move this food to the cup. Record your results on the chart.

Birds and Their Beaks

1. The bird I've chosen is the:————————————————————————————

2. What this bird eats: ————————————————————————————————

——

3. My sketch of the bird's beak:

57

4. Materials I've used to make a model of the beak:

_____

5. Have a partner time you for one minute while you use your beak to pick up as many food items as you can. Then record the kinds and numbers of "foods" at this station your beak was able to pick up in one minute.

Kinds of Food	How Many My Beak Collected

Conclusions:

1. What type of food(s) is your bird best adapted to capturing? _____

_____

2. Is your bird beak better adapted to eating one type of food or several types of food? Why? _____

_____

3. How would you change your bird beak to make it better at capturing food?_____

_____

_____

Challenge: What would your bird do if the food it is best adapted to capturing was destroyed?_____

_____

_____

_____

ACTIVITY SHEET

12d

STATION RECORD SHEET
STATION 4

Problem: How does a shark's sense of smell help it to detect its prey in the ocean?

Procedure: (1) Smell each of the seven jars one at at time. (2) Describe what you smell, guess what the substance is, and mark whether or not this could be human "prey." (3) Answer the questions at the bottom of this sheet.

Jar	Describe What You Smell	Record Your Guess	Is This Human Prey? (Yes or No)
1			
2			
3			
4			
5			
6			
7			

Questions:

1. Share your results with your team. How many times did your group have the same guess?_____ Does your team have similar or different abilities to identify odors? Explain.

_____

2. Some animals use their sense of smell to find food. Has your sense of smell ever alerted you to the presence of food? Explain. _____

_____

3. Many forest animals use their sense of smell to detect danger. How might humans use their sense of smell to detect danger? _____

_____

4. Which of your five senses do you depend upon the most? Explain your answer. _____

_____

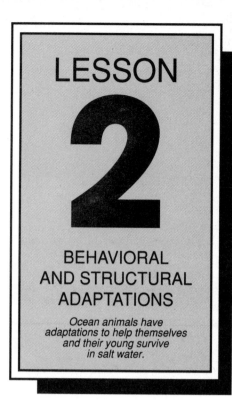

LESSON 2

BEHAVIORAL AND STRUCTURAL ADAPTATIONS

Ocean animals have adaptations to help themselves and their young survive in salt water.

2. For each group performing the demonstrations you will need:
   - Copies of Activity Sheets 13a-13c
   - 2 strips of white construction paper, food coloring, vaseline, a bowl filled with water
   - 1 eggplant, 1 cucumber, 1 apple (other fruit may be substituted), knife (to be used by the teacher), plastic plates or waxed paper, salt
   - thermometer, paper cups, bowl, warm water, icy salt water, a variety of insulators—blubber: vaseline or lard; skin: plastic wrap or aluminum foil; fur: wool sock or material
3. Reference materials
4. Writing and art materials

LESSON OUTLINE

Before the lesson begins:

1. Duplicate Activity Sheets 13a-13c (one set for each student).
2. Collect copies of *Zoobooks* and other reference materials.
3. Purchase materials listed under "YOU NEED" for the three demonstrations.

During the lesson:

1. Follow the lesson steps to have students
   (a) Brainstorm for prior understanding of ocean conditions, how ocean water affects human skin, ways ocean conditions may cause problems for aquatic life, how humans protect themselves from the effects of ocean water, and how animals protect themselves from these same effects.
   (b) Define the terms STRUCTURAL and BEHAVIORAL.
   (c) Complete the three demonstration activities.
   (d) Work in groups to research both structural and behavioral adaptations their animal possesses to protect itself and to care for its young.
   (e) Continue with their unit projects, Ocean Journals, reading, and portfolios.

60

INTRODUCTION

Students brainstorm for prior knowledge by identifying conditions in the ocean, describing what happens when they stay in water too long, and writing sentences telling how ocean conditions can create problems for living things. Students then define structural and behavioral adaptations. Students investigate these two types of adaptations in three demonstration activities. Next, students work in cooperative learning groups to conduct research on how an ocean animal protects and cares for its young. Finally, students integrate these ideas into their unit projects.

OBJECTIVES:

1. To investigate the structural adaptations that protect ocean animals from specific elements in their environment
2. To research and present behavioral adaptations that ocean animals use to protect their young

YOU NEED:

1. Copies of the eight *Zoobooks* in this module

(f) Continue to collect reading resources about animal adaptations.

2. Words to add to your **Classroom Glossary:**

  Structural adaptation

  Behavioral adaptation

  Offspring

STEP 1:

Brainstorming for Prior Knowledge

Invite students to brainstorm plant, animal, and nonliving things as well as specific conditions, like temperature, that are found in an ocean environment. Write their suggestions on the chalkboard. Discuss what happens when people stay in water a long time. (Their skin wrinkles.) Guide students to draw the conclusion that water affects our skin. Invite students to brainstorm other ways ocean water affects things in it. Then ask students to form small groups. Have each group choose three or four of the items on the class list. For each item they've chosen, have them write a sentence that tells how this item could create a problem for an animal living in the ocean. (Examples: cold water lowering body temperature so much that it kills an animal; large fish getting tangled up in seaweed.) Invite students to list adaptations that help animals avoid or solve the problem.

STEP 2:

Defining Terms: <u>Structural</u> and <u>Behavioral</u>

On the chalkboard, write the words "structure" and "behavior." Review the definition of structural adaptation you discussed with the class in Lesson 1. Invite students to define or describe what they think the "structure" of an animal is and give examples from the list created at the end of Step 1. (Structure is the form and functions that the animal has no control over.) They might choose items like wing size, blubber, or feathers. Invite students to tell all the ways people adapt to changing weather. Have them identify those that are structural adaptations. Shivering and sweating

are examples; however, most adaptations the students name will not be structural.

Next, invite students to tell everything they know about the term "behavior." Explain that when the word "behavior" is used with the term "adaptation," it means a change in the way animals act or behave so that they can better deal with their environment. Ask which of the adaptations humans make to weather are behavioral. (Most will be.) Ask students to identify some ocean animal adaptations that are behavioral, such as an otter floating on its back or a seabird sitting on a nest. Suggest that students work independently to create one list of structural adaptations and another of behavioral adaptations for humans and animals. Then students can work with a partner to evaluate their lists and defend or correct each entry.

61

This activity can be extended by comparing human and animal thinking. The most important difference is that humans have special problem-solving abilities. Invite students to compare how animals and humans solve specific problems, such as hunger.

STEP 3:

Investigating Structural and Behavioral Adaptations

Estimated time: 1-2 class periods

In this activity, students investigate different ways animals meet their needs through structural and behavioral adaptations. The three demonstrations can be done by the whole class, by small groups, or by partners or individuals. Set up group stations or a demonstration area, or pass out materials to students.

DEMONSTRATION 1

PROBLEM: Why do some ocean animals have oil on their feathers and fur?

Procedure: Ask students to use two strips of white construction paper, liberally smear vaseline all over the end of one strip, then dip both strips into colored water. Invite students to describe what happens and state their conclusion: Though some water may seep through, the vaseline (oil) generally protects an animal from the water. Ask students to suggest examples of behavioral and structural adaptations that some animals might have to ensure that the oil remains effective, like birds preening their feathers. Invite students to answer the question: *"What structural or behavioral adaptations do saltwater animals need that freshwater animals do not need?"* (One example—sea otters groom themselves to trap air bubbles in their fur, insulating their skin from the water.)

DEMONSTRATION 2

PROBLEM: How does salt water affect ocean life?

Procedure: Cut several different fruits and vegetables vertically, so that some slices are covered with the skin and other slices have exposed flesh (eggplant, cucumber, and apples work very well). Place the slices on plastic plates or waxed paper so that some slices have only the skin facing up and others have the exposed flesh facing up. Ask students to predict what will happen to the slices if they are sprinkled with salt. Discuss predictions.

Then sprinkle salt on the slices and allow to sit for 30 minutes.

Leave the slices where students can observe them. After 30 minutes, have students note the water that has appeared on the exposed flesh of the vegetables. Ask why the slices covered with skin do not have as much water. (The skin protects the water in the flesh and prevents it from being drawn out by the salt.) Ask students how ocean organisms protect themselves from the salt in the ocean.

DEMONSTRATION 3

PROBLEM: How can ocean animals insulate themselves against the ocean's cold water?

Procedure: Tell students that the cups of warm water represent ocean mammals. Discuss how the mammal keeps itself warm in cold water. Have students look at pictures in *Zoobooks* to give them ideas. Show students the materials available (vaseline or lard) to insulate the cups (mammals). Ask each group to plan how it will use the materials to keep its mammal warm (maintain the same temperature). After all of the groups have carried out their plans, fill the paper cups with warm water and place them in the bowls filled with ice water. Place a paper cup that has not been insulated into another bowl of ice water to act as a control. Have each group record the temperature of its insulated cup every three minutes. After 15 minutes, share the temperatures with the class. Have each group share the results and ask the class to identify the most effective insulating system. Compare this to the insulating systems of real mammals. Invite students to suggest examples of behavioral and structural adaptations that could protect ocean animals from cold temperatures, such as blubber and thick fur.

CONCLUSION:
Discuss the investigations with students. Invite them to recall structural and behavioral adaptations that help sea animals deal with the water, temperature, and salt in their environment.

Ask individuals or small groups to skim their *Zoobooks* to find at least two examples of how ocean animals keep water, temperature, and salt from harming them. Have them identify whether each is a structural or behavioral adaptation.

They can write this information in their Ocean Journals.

STEP 4:
Focusing on the Young of Ocean Animals

This is a jigsaw cooperative learning activity. Students form groups of eight students each. (Group size can be smaller if fewer *Zoobooks* titles are used.) Each member of the group chooses a different *Zoobook* to study. New groups are formed, with all those students who have chosen the same *Zoobook* meeting together to become "experts" on the structures and behaviors their animal species uses to care for its young. (Note: There is a wide variety among different species. For example, turtles and sharks do not provide as much care as birds or mammals.)

With the information students gather during their investigation of the *Zoobooks* and other research material, they create a time line that shows the care the parents give to their young throughout that species' childhood. Once the groups have completed their research, they discuss the important ideas and write three or more questions they feel every student should be able to answer about this topic. Once you've collected these questions, compile and edit them into a worksheet of questions from every group.

After completing their research, discussion, and questions, students return to their original group. Each member is responsible for teaching the other members about the animal they've become an "expert" on. Each group creates a chart comparing the information from each of its members. To continue this evaluation, groups can compare their charts to make sure all have the same pertinent information. Finally, ask all students to complete the worksheet you created.

STEP 5:
Continuing the Unit Projects

Remind students to include in their unit projects behavioral adaptations that enable their animal to protect itself and its young from salt water. Suggest that as they work on their projects they check to make sure they have displayed a variety of structural and behavioral adaptations.

ECOCONNECTION ACTIVITY

Encourage students to observe and identify the structures and behaviors that the living things in the aquarium use to protect themselves from the seawater or freshwater. If desired, obtain frog eggs or fish eggs which are suited to your aquarium so students can observe the life cycle. If studying a terrarium or mini-ecosystem, have students look for structures and behaviors that the living things have to protect themselves from heat, cold, or rain.

CURRICULUM CONNECTIONS
Music and Poetry: Writing Ocean Songs

Play a few lullabies, such as "All the Pretty Little Horses" or "Deep Blue Sea," or read poems such as Rudyard Kipling's "The Seal Lullaby" to your students. Discuss how the words and rhythm reflect particular surroundings. Examine the imagery and discuss how it might appeal to young children. Then invite students to choose one ocean animal and write a song, lullaby, or poem that the adult animals might sing to their young. The composition should include details about the animal's natural surroundings. It might also warn of dangers, describe behaviors the adult uses to protect itself from predators or the ocean

63

environment, or tell about food sources. Have students tape their songs and share them with the class.

Anthropology:
Human Adaptations

Have students work in small groups to study how humans in different cultures have changed their behavior to adapt to different environments. Each group researches how a culture or civilization conducted the basic activities of human civilization. These activities are marketplace, transportation, communication, protection, education, tools / technology, recreation, organization/government, moral/ethical/religious, and esthetic. You may want to simplify them for your class as follows: food, transportation, housing, clothing, recreation, defense, religion, tools, art, music, and sports. Have each team present its findings to the class. Students can then compare these cultures to each other and to our culture. Ask the class how the environment (climate, types of resources available, etc.) has affected the culture's adaptations.

Other students can investigate how people change their behavior to adapt to new situations. They can brainstorm events that cause change in our daily life (examples: weather, divorce, or winning the lottery) and ways that people adapt to these changes. They can investigate what psychologists say about how people adapt to problems and changes in their lives, such as natural disasters like hurricanes. Invite students to create skits or stories to illustrate some of their findings and present them to the class.

Dance:
Animals in Motion

Suggest that a group of students choose several ocean animals and create an ocean dance based on their movement and interaction in the sea. They can use lighting and props to simulate an ocean environment and choose music that fits the mood of the behaviors they are dancing.

Preparing for the next lesson

Encourage students to make additional cards for the Memory Game to add to the ones created in Lesson 1. Have students update their portfolio Table of Contents. Suggest they include their Curriculum Connections materials and a list of all the different adaptations they've learned about so far. Now might be a good time to have students confer with you or with a study partner about whether their portfolios are helping them reach their learning goals.

ACTIVITY SHEET

13a

Surviving in Ocean Waters

DEMONSTRATION 1

1. Predict what will happen when you dip both strips of paper into the colored water.

Plain paper: _____

Paper with vaseline: _____

2. Observe what happens when you dip each strip into the water, and write your observations here.

65

Plain paper: _____

Paper with vaseline: _____

3. What can you conclude from this activity?_____

_____

_____

4. What are some behavioral and structural adaptations that some animals have to keep natural oils effective?

_____

_____

_____

_____

5. What are some structural or behavioral adaptations saltwater animals need that freshwater animals do not?

_____

_____

_____

_____

ACTIVITY SHEET

13b

Surviving in Ocean Waters

DEMONSTRATION 2

1. Predict what will happen to the slices that are sprinkled with salt.

_____

_____

_____

_____

2. Record your observations after 30 minutes.

_____

_____

_____

_____

3. What can you conclude from this activity?

_____

_____

_____

_____

4. How can ocean animals protect themselves from the salt in the ocean?

_____

_____

_____

EXPLORING OCEAN ECOSYSTEMS

ACTIVITY SHEET

13c

Surviving in Ocean Waters

1. Explain how you will use the materials to insulate your cup so that the temperature will remain the same.

_____

_____

2. Draw a picture of your plan.

67

3. Record the temperature readings below:

					Group				
	1	2	3	4	5	6	7	8	Control
Temperature									

4. Which insulation method was most effective? Why?_____

_____

_____

5. What are some structural and behavioral adaptations that could protect ocean animals from cold temperatures?

_____

_____

LESSON 3

PROTECTIVE ADAPTATIONS

Ocean animals have adaptations to protect themselves from predators.

68

INTRODUCTION

Students begin investigating protective adaptations by brainstorming ways animals and people protect themselves. They then use the *Zoobooks* to observe and define camouflage as a type of structural adaptation. Students further observe how light affects camouflage by observing three light demonstrations. As part of the third demonstration, students create their own colorful fish and wear goggles to simulate underwater lighting conditions. Wearing the goggles, students act as predators and capture the fish. Students then infer which type of coloration provided the most effective camouflage. In the next step, students go on an adaptations "scavenger hunt" using *Zoobooks* to find the answers. Finally, students complete work on their unit projects.

OBJECTIVES:

1. To investigate the relationship between light, water depth, and camouflage
2. To identify specific structural and behavioral adaptations of ocean animals that protect them from predators

YOU NEED:

1. Copies of the eight *Zoobooks* in this module
2. For the science investigation:
   - prism
   - white construction paper
   - cardboard (with a slit for light to come through) cut to fit into a slide projector
   - slide projector
   - Three 4" x 7" pieces of blue cellophane per student (obtainable from an art supply store in larger sheets that you can cut down to size)
   - aquarium with water
   - string
   - pattern for goggles (Activity Sheet 14) printed on heavy paper
3. For the cooperative learning activity, Activity Sheet 15—Scavenger Hunt (3 pages)
4. Writing and art materials

LESSON OUTLINE

Before the lesson begins:

1. Obtain the materials for the three light demonstration activities and try them before you perform them for the students.
2. Purchase and cut the blue cellophane, duplicate the goggles pattern on heavy paper, and make sample goggles to show students.
3. Gather a variety of construction paper colors, scissors, and glue to be used to make the fish.
4. Duplicate one copy of *Zoobooks* Scavenger Hunt (Activity Sheet 15) per student.

During the lesson:

1. Follow the lesson steps to
   (a) Brainstorm for prior knowledge of ways animals and humans protect themselves.
   (b) Define the term CAMOUFLAGE.

2. Words to add to your **Classroom Glossary:**
   Protection
   Camouflage
   Intensity
   Prism
   Spectrum
   Absorbed

STEP 1:

Brainstorming for Prior Knowledge

Brainstorm a chalkboard list of ways that animals and people protect themselves. Be sure students include ideas such as flee, fight, and hide. Invite students to illustrate or act out some of their ideas.

STEP 2:

Defining Terms: Camouflage

Invite students to describe a penguin. As you list their suggestions, circle "white underside." Ask students what else is white in a penguin's environment (snow and ice). Show the *Zoobook* picture of penguins swimming under ice and discuss how the penguin blends into its surroundings of bright, white ice for protection.

Write CAMOUFLAGE on the chalkboard and explain that the penguin blending into its surroundings is an example of camouflage.

Ask students if they think the purpose of a sea turtle's shell or a shark's teeth is camouflage. (A shark's tooth is not camouflage. The color of the turtle's shell *is* camouflage, but the shell does more than camouflage the turtle—it also protects it.) Ask students to give other examples of camouflage. Encourage them to write a working definition of camouflage in this context, then to look up the word in the dictionary. Most dictionaries have more than one definition. Ask students to choose the one that is most appropriate and then use it to evaluate their working definition. Encourage students to use *Zoobooks* to provide more examples of camouflage and other protective structures and behaviors that are not camouflage.

STEP 3:

Investigating Camouflage and Light

69

> Estimated time: 2 class periods

In this investigation students will explore the color or colors that are most effective in camouflaging fish in the ocean. The investigation begins with three demonstrations showing how light intensity (quantity or brightness) and quality (colors present) are affected when light passes through different amounts of water. Students then apply this knowledge in a simulation activity. To set the stage for the demonstrations, first review the properties of light. The extent of this discussion will depend on your students' prior knowledge. Emphasize the difference between the intensity (brightness) of light and its quality (the colors present). Other concepts the class might discuss are reflection, refraction, diffusion, dispersion, wavelengths, white light, and how distance affects the brightness of light.

For each of the demonstrations, present the problem, ask students to make predictions, enlist students to help carry out the demonstration, and conclude by asking students to verify or change their predictions. **CAUTION:** The results are based on human perceptions, so different people will see different things.

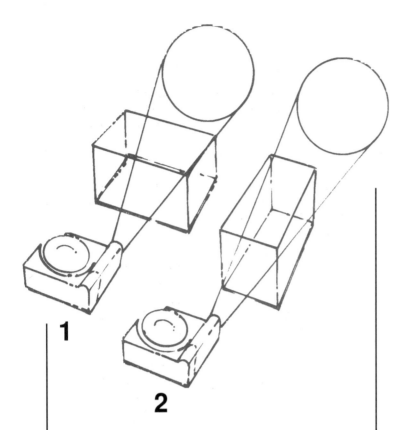

1

2

You may get several different answers, which can lead to a lively discussion about the reliability of a theory based only on human perception.

CAUTION: Move the aquarium when it is empty. Fill it with clean water when it is in place for the demonstrations.

DEMONSTRATION 1

PROBLEM: What colors make up white light?

Procedure: Darken the classroom and turn on the projector. Put a prism in the light between the projector and white paper until a color spectrum is projected onto the white paper. Encourage students to identify the colors that make up the white light, as shown in the spectrum (red, orange, yellow, green, blue, indigo, and violet).

DEMONSTRATION 2

PROBLEM: Is the intensity (brightness) of light lost when it passes through water?

Procedure: Shine the projector's light through the short side of the aquarium (see illustration 1 above) onto the white paper. Then do the same thing through the long side of the aquarium (see illustration 2). Have students compare which light is brighter and hypothesize why. (The shorter the distance through the water, the brighter the light.)

DEMONSTRATION 3

PROBLEM: Does the quality of light (colors present) change when it passes through water?

Procedure: Place the cardboard slide in the projector to focus the light beam. Shine the projector's light through the prism and then through the water onto white paper. Have students determine if some colors are brighter than others. If necessary, compare the spectrums created both before and after the light has gone through the water. (Red and yellow are absorbed faster than other colors when light passes through water.) As students discuss the three demonstrations and draw conclusions, ascertain that they understand that light is absorbed (the quantity is decreased) as it passes through water, but that some colors (red and yellow) are absorbed sooner than others (blue). Have students predict what color will be seen in fairly deep waters where much light has been absorbed (blue) versus what color will be seen in the deepest parts of the ocean. (No color, because all light has been absorbed. People must bring their own light.)

SIMULATION—OCEAN LIGHT

1. Invite each student to create a fish out of colored construction paper. Be sure students use a variety of colors. Ask students to write their names on the back of their fish. Then collect the fish. Hold up several fish and ask students to predict which are best camouflaged for the classroom. Have students explain their answers. Next, ask students to predict how the fish would look different underwater. Ask which of the fish is best camouflaged for an underwater environment.

2. Discuss the characteristics of the deepest parts of the ocean where light still reaches. Call on a volunteer to suggest why the light found there might be simulated by using goggles made of blue cellophane. Distribute Activity Sheet 14 and model with students how to make the goggles. As students make their goggles, explain that they will be sent out of the room so you can hide the fish and that when they return, they will wear the goggles to simulate the ocean light and will act as predators to capture the fish. Then tell them

to take their goggles with them when they leave the classroom.

3. While students are out of the classroom, arrange the fish around the room. Put them against dark backgrounds—for example, on bulletin boards or shelves or in corners and open closets. Pull down the window shades to create a dim light similar to the light found underwater. Use a pair of goggles to check that some fish disappear into their background. This happens when the fish and the background have the same color value. Seen through the goggles, reds and yellows will have the same values as browns and grays.

4. As students return to the classroom, tell them to put their goggles on to help them

see as if they were in a deep part of the ocean. Remind them that while they are wearing the goggles they should pretend to be predators. Tell them to try to locate as many of the fish as possible and, once located, to identify what color they are without removing the goggles. Remind students of their predictions about what colors can be seen at different depths in the ocean. Explain that they will have only three minutes to "capture" (identify and count) as many "prey" (fish) as they can.

CAUTION: Some people see an afterimage after wearing the goggles for more than five minutes. (This phenomenon is similar to what happens after you have your picture taken with a flash camera.) Reassure students by explaining that this afterimage occurs because the brain has adjusted to the blue goggles and must readjust to full light. This condition will clear up quickly and does not cause any permanent changes in the eye or vision.

5. After students remove their goggles, ask them to compare their findings with the "real" colors of the fish. (Red and yellow will look brownish; only blue will seem true.) Have them speculate about why certain colors were difficult or impossible to

see. (They blended into the background and most colors were similar.) As reinforcement, repeat the activity with no goggles or with a different color of cellophane in the goggles.

CONCLUSION:

Discuss the results with students. Have them generalize and reassess their predictions (which of the fish are best camouflaged for an underwater environment) using their results. Invite them to predict how what they saw differs from what they'd see on the deepest ocean floor. (They'd see nothing; no light penetrates that far.) Ask them to speculate on what explorers saw when they brought lights into the darkest parts of the ocean. (A variety of colorful, white, and gray creatures.) Have students suggest other ways animals are camouflaged besides by color (examples: textures that blend into surroundings; shapes that fool predators). Suggest students create illustrations of deep-sea life, including camouflaged animals.

71

STEP 4:
Focusing on Camouflage and Other Adaptations

Estimated time: 4-5 class periods

Have students return to their cooperative learning groups. Each group will be responsible for finding the answers to the scavenger hunt questions and locating the camouflaged animal. They can divide the work so that each member finds the answers to certain questions, or group members can work together on the entire puzzle.

Hand out the three pages of Activity Sheet 15. Explain that students will use the *Zoobooks* to hunt for specific facts.

Before groups begin the scavenger hunt, you may want to review the following skimming strategy by reminding students to

- <u>Read</u> the question carefully.
- <u>Identify</u> the topic and key words.
- <u>Determine</u> which book or books might cover the topic.
- <u>Skim</u> the book to find the key words in the text or the pictures.

- Reread the question carefully.
- Read the text and observe pictures carefully to locate the correct answer.

Once the facts are located in the *Zoobooks*, students should follow the specific coloring directions. When the activity is done correctly, a fish will be revealed. A more complete evaluation can be done by discussing students' answers. To help them develop metacognitive learning strategies (their thought processes as answers were found), invite students to explain how they arrived at their answers.

Students can use the details from the scavenger hunt to create cards for their Memory Game. Suggest they include at least two pairs that show adaptations which allow sea animals to escape predators (camouflage, speed, spines, etc.).

STEP 5:
Finalizing the Unit Projects

Remind students to include information about camouflage and other protective adaptations in their unit projects. As they complete their projects, have students check to make sure that all their depictions of animal adaptations are accurate.

ECOCONNECTION ACTIVITY

Have students observe the plants and animals in their aquarium, terrarium, or mini-ecosystem to look for examples of camouflage or other protective behaviors.

CURRICULUM CONNECTIONS

Music:
Themes

Discuss the way a specific melody could be camouflaged within a larger piece of music.

A good example is Mozart's Variations on *"Ah! Vous dirai-je, Maman."* This takes the melody that we know as "Twinkle, Twinkle, Little Star" through various modifications. It is available from recording companies such as Music and Art and CBS . To expand on the lesson, set up a listening center and invite interested students to listen for a musical theme in classical or movie music (such as *Superman* or *Doctor Zhivago*) and identifythe theme every time it appears in complete, abbreviated, or modified form.

Writing:
Point of View

Have students research some of the U.S. Navy's deepwater experiments such as humans living underwater or using small submarines for exploration. Have them write letters or journal entries from the point of view of Navy scientists conducting the investigations. Suggest that students include information about what they see, think, and feel. They might also write about their problems, fears, and discoveries as investigators.

Art:
Visual Puzzles

Introduce students to visual puzzles that depend on perception, not visual acuity, such as the faces-or-vase picture at right, or hidden pictures, such as those found in children's activity books. Encourage students to draw their own hidden picture showing how an animal can hide itself in its habitat. Students can use *Zoobooks* and other references to learn how an animal hides from predators. For more complicated optical illusions, show students Escher's drawings, such as *Up and Down,* which shows a never-ending staircase. Challenge students to create their own visual puzzles or optical illusions relating to the ocean. Simple visual puzzles can be shared with younger students and more complex ones with their own classmates.

Literature: Myths, Fairy Tales, and Folktales

Invite students to recall or find and then retell myths, fairy tales, or folktales that have beings which take on different forms or disguises, such as a frog or coyote that turns into a human. After retelling the tales, discuss the answers to questions such as: "Why does the character have these different forms?" "How does the tale reflect the culture it comes from?" "What lesson is the tale trying to teach?" "What similarities are there among tales from different cultures?" Then suggest that students write their own tales about humans transformed into ocean animals or vice versa. Invite students to share their tales with the class.

UNIT WIND-UP AND ASSESSMENT

1. Ask small groups of students to review their unit findings to respond to the problem posed in Lesson 1: "*How do structural and behavioral adaptations help ocean animals survive?*" Bring the class together to discuss the groups' responses and create a class list that all students can agree to. Invite students to expand the problem to land animals and discuss how they adapt, structurally and behaviorally, to their environment. Then describe a very different environment from the one students are used to and have them tell how people might adapt to it: What structures would they need that are different from those they use now? What behavioral adaptations would they make?

2. Schedule presentations of the unit projects. Beforehand, develop with the class a set of criteria the students will use when assessing their own and other unit projects. (For ideas on criteria, see the *Teaching Strategies* Supplement.) After the presentations, display the projects for everyone to examine. Invite other classes in to see them, too.

3. Ask students to complete their Ocean Animal Adaptations Portfolios. Suggest they include a Table of Contents, completed investigations and group activities, and any Curriculum Connections materials. They might also include photocopies of some pairs of cards from their Memory Game. Invite students to choose their two favorite activities from the unit and edit and recopy them so they can be placed on display in the classroom. Ask students to write entries in their journals telling why they especially enjoyed these activities.

Meet with students individually or in groups and have them evaluate their portfolios and discuss how they reflect what the students learned during the unit. Invite them to tell how their knowledge has grown because of the activities in which they participated.

4. Encourage students to add adaptations they've investigated in this lesson to their card decks. After they complete their decks, they can play the Memory Game, which concludes this unit.

Procedure:
1. After forming into cooperative learning groups, students explain to group members each card and its relationship to its mate. Besides being an evaluation tool, this step will help to clarify details in individual pictures.
2. Students then shuffle the deck and place each card face down in rows on the desk.
3. Each student takes a turn turning over two cards. If the cards match (animal activity and adaptation), that player keeps the cards. If the cards don't match, they are turned over again in the exact location in which they were found. The goal is to remember where cards are so that students can match cards they uncover with ones they've already seen.
4. The game continues until all cards are matched. The winner is the player with the most cards. Groups can trade decks and play the game with the unfamiliar cards. As a special challenge, the class can play the game with all the cards. The cards can also be used to play a version of "Go Fish." Invite students to create their own games, including written rules, and to try out all the games their classmates have invented.

SEE
UNDER THE
SEA

74

Trace this goggle pattern onto heavy paper and cut it out. Cut out the eye holes and tape three layers of blue cellophane over them. Attach loops of string to the side holes on the goggles. Put these loops around your ears to hold the goggles in place.

Exploring Ocean Ecosystems

ACTIVITY SHEET

15

Zoobooks Scavenger Hunt

Use your *Zoobooks* and follow these directions. If you follow them correctly, you will uncover the camouflaged animal hiding in the picture on the last page of this Activity.

1. If a penguin's bones and body shape are better adapted to flying, color (A) — **BLUE**. If a penguin's bones and body shape are better adapted to swimming, color (A) — *YELLOW*.

2. If a penguin's swimming speed is a little faster than a human's swimming speed, color all the (B) spaces **Brown**. If it is a lot faster than a human's swimming speed, color them **BLUE**.

3. If the following sentence is true, color all the (C) spaces **Brown**. If it is false, color them **BLUE**. *Frigatebirds eat and sleep while flying.*

4. Read the list of factors below. Color the spaces **BLUE** that are factors which help seabirds fly:
   (D) hollow, lightweight bones
   (E) short legs
   (F) oil on their feathers
   (G) webbed feet
   (H) a small body in relation to their wings

5. Color (I) the color that follows the correct answer to this question: *What is the most important use of the sea otter's flexible spine?*
   to play games and wrestle—**BLUE**
   to catch its food—**Brown**
   to keep its fur clean—*YELLOW*
   to swim—*Green*

6. Color *YELLOW* all the spaces that correctly complete this sentence: *While cleaning their fur, sea otters:*
   (J) pull their coat around to reach all spots.
   (K) use their sharp claws as a comb.
   (L) use their forepaws to press out the water.
   (M) add air next to their skin by rubbing hard and blowing on their fur.
   (N) pull out lots of old hairs to make room for new hairs.

75

7. Color ⓞ the color listed after the correct ending to this sentence:
Sharks get oxygen:

> as whales do, through airholes— YELLOW

> as fish do, through gills—**BLUE**

8. Color all the Ⓟ spaces the color listed after the best ending to this sentence: *If we compare a shark's brain to a human brain, we can find out:*

> why sharks are so hungry all the time— YELLOW

> how much more important the sense of smell is to sharks—**Brown**

> why sharks' heads are round—**BLUE**

9. Color all the Ⓠ spaces the color listed after the best ending for this sentence: *A great white shark takes a big bite out of its prey by:*

> rotating its jaws forward—**BLUE**

> unhinging its jaws—**Brown**

> sneaking up behind its prey— YELLOW

10. Color all the Ⓡ spaces the color listed after the best answer to this question: *What differentiates the two main groups of whales?*

> their body shapes— YELLOW

> how they catch their food—**BLUE**

> how they breathe—Red

11. Color all the Ⓢ spaces the color listed after the best ending to this sentence: *The whale gets power to move through the water by:*

> moving its tail up and down—Red

> pushing and pulling with its flippers— YELLOW

> moving its tail side to side—**BLUE**

12. Color Ⓣ the color listed after the best ending to this sentence: *Whales must come to the surface often to:*

> breathe air— YELLOW

> find food—**BLUE**

> see where they're going—Red

13. Color Ⓤ the color listed after the best answer to this question: *If it is hard to see anything underwater, how do whales locate things?*

> sense of smell—**BLUE**

> echo-location—**Brown**

> extremely sensitive eyes that need no light to see— YELLOW

14. If walrus use their tusks for killing large animals for their food, color all the Ⓥ spaces YELLOW. If they use them for finding food on the ocean bottom, color the Ⓥ spaces **BLUE**.

15. If a sea turtle's shell protects every part of its body, color Ⓦ— YELLOW. If it does not protect all of its body, color Ⓦ—**BLUE**.

16. Color all the Ⓧ spaces the color listed after the best ending to this sentence: *Sea turtles and sharks are alike because:*

> they haven't changed much since the days of dinosaurs—**Brown**

> they protect themselves with shells—**BLUE**

76

17. Color Ⓨthe color listed after the best ending to this sentence: *Otters and penguins are different because:*

      they have different adaptations to keep warm— *Yellow*

      one is cold-blooded and one is warm-blooded— Red

      one never comes out of the water—**Brown**

18. Color Ⓩthe color listed after the best answer to this question: *How are gulls and otters alike?*

      They swim long distances underwater— Red

      They crack shells to get to shellfish— *Yellow*

      They go for days without eating—**Brown**

If you have followed the directions correctly, you will uncover the camouflaged animal hiding in this picture.

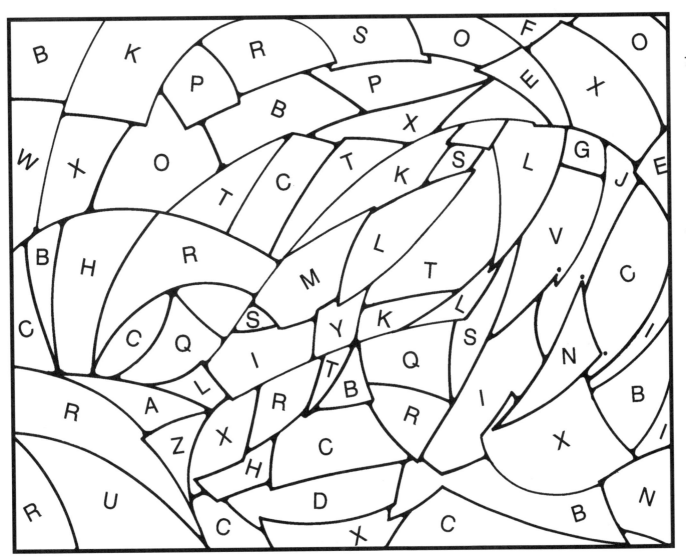

77

UNIT 3

Humans and the Ocean Ecosystems

Unit Concept:

HUMANS ARE INTERDEPENDENT PARTS OF THE OCEAN ECOSYSTEMS.

- *We depend on the ocean for many of our needs.*

- *Our interaction with ocean ecosystems affects the living and nonliving parts of the ocean.*

- *We have the responsibility to ensure that our actions do not harm the ocean ecosystems.*

LESSON

1

DEPENDING ON THE OCEAN

We depend on the ocean for many of our needs.

Oceans Disappear

INTRODUCTION

Students begin the unit on human dependence on the ocean by completing a pre-assessment Idea Web. They brainstorm possible consequences to humans if our oceans were to disappear. Students then define the term "resource" and identify ways humans use the ocean as a resource to meet their needs. Students form news teams to research and create a news show on the ways humans use the ocean. Next, students use *Zoobooks* to identify how human uses of the ocean may affect ocean animals. Finally, students brainstorm and begin work on a unit project.

OBJECTIVES:

1. To investigate human uses of the ocean
2. To investigate some impacts of human use on the ocean ecosystems

YOU NEED:

1. Copies of the eight *Zoobooks* in this module
2. For the science investigation:
   • copies of Activity Sheet 16
   • additional reference materials listed in Lesson Step 3
3. For the cooperative learning activity, copies of Activity Sheet 17 (2 pages)
4. Writing and art materials
5. VCR and TV, and (optional) camcorder and tripod

LESSON OUTLINE

Before the lesson begins:

1. Gather the reference materials for Step 3.
2. Videotape a news show or select one to have students watch for homework.
3. Duplicate Activity Sheets 16 and 17 for each student.
4. Obtain a camcorder and videotape if you want students to videotape their news show.

During the lesson:

1. Follow the lesson steps to have students
   (a) Complete the pre-assessment.
   (b) Brainstorm for prior knowledge of human dependence upon the ocean.

(c) Define the term RESOURCE.

(d) Research and create a news show on how humans use the ocean.

(e) Use *Zoobooks* to identify ways that human uses of the ocean affect ocean animals.

(f) Begin their unit projects. (**Note:** As you discuss ideas for the unit projects with students, develop criteria with them to evaluate those projects. Refer to page 17 in the *Teaching Strategies* Supplement for ideas on how to do this.)

2. Have students continue to add to their Ocean Journals.

3. Have students create a new portfolio for this unit titled Human Interaction with the Ocean.

4. Direct students to look for and collect materials from magazines, newspapers, and other reading sources that give information about current topics concerning how humans use the ocean to meet their needs.

5. Have students select reading material they will read throughout the unit. Students can find appropriate materials in the bibliography at the end of this Curriculum Guide or from the card catalog or computer in the library.

6. Words to add to your **Classroom Glossary**:

   Resource

PRE- AND POST-ASSESSMENT

Distribute a sheet of paper and ask students to draw an Idea Web showing how humans interact with, and depend upon, the ocean. The web should include lines, arrows, and words describing the interaction. Students may add drawings to illustrate their ideas.

Review the Idea Webs to look for ideas students already understand and misconceptions they may hold. Return the webs to students to place in their portfolios. At the end of the unit, have students make another web. Comparing the two webs can be one post-assessment method.

81

STEP 1:

Brainstorming for Prior Knowledge

Ahead of time, prepare a streamer headline to display prominently: OCEANS DISAPPEAR IN COSMIC ACCIDENT! Invite students to brainstorm and list on the chalkboard newspaper headlines that would follow the banner announcing this fantastic cataclysmic event. Students will probably first suggest headlines such as ALL LIFE IN THE SEA DESTROYED. Ask students to go on to headlines that announce the impact on human beings. Examples are VITAL FOOD SOURCE GONE; CLIMATE AND WEATHER PATTERNS CHANGE RADICALLY; FISHING FLEETS NO LONGER NEEDED; MAJOR MODE OF TRANSPORTATION IS HISTORY; BEACH HOUSES FACE DRY LAND; ART LOVERS SCRAMBLE FOR PAINTINGS OF VANISHED SEA; DESALINATION PLANTS GRIND TO A HALT—MILLIONS THIRSTY.

Conclude the brainstorming by inviting students to list questions they hope the unit will answer about human dependence on the ocean and the ocean ecosystems. Keep the lists of headlines and students' questions on display.

STEP 2:

Defining Terms: <u>Resource</u>

On the chalkboard, write RESOURCES. Remind students that humans (like all living things) interact with their environment to meet their needs. Ask students to list the resources humans depend upon to meet their needs and what needs those resources supply. If students do not suggest the ocean, ask students if the ocean is a <u>resource</u> humans depend upon. Encourage students to realize that oceans stabilize climate as well as provide food, transportation routes, oil and minerals, water, energy, and recreation. In addition, ocean plants provide oxygen to the environment.

A PROBLEM TO SOLVE: Write the following question on poster paper for display: "*In what ways can humans use the ocean ecosystems without harming them?*" Explain that as students work through this unit they will gather material that will help them to solve this problem. To build on previous knowledge, the class might make a related generalization based on what they have learned in your social studies program about wise use of land. Suggest that students begin their solutions to this particular problem by listing their questions and concerns about human use of the ocean, and then making this list a preamble page for their portfolios for this unit.

STEP 3:

Investigating Human Uses of the Ocean

Estimated time: 3-5 class periods

This investigation helps students to gather in-depth information on the different ways humans use the ocean to meet their needs. Students use a variety of sources to gather information about goals, technology, cultural similarities and differences, and other topics the students identify. Students will use the results of their investigation in a news show like "60 Minutes." They'll also refer to the results of the investigation as they work in cooperative learning groups (Step 4).

Procedure:
1. Give students an overview of the lesson. Invite students to help you find and organize the resource materials for the activity. In addition to general and nature encyclopedias, the *Zoobooks*, other periodicals, and pertinent nonfiction books from your library, have on hand in a central location the following kinds of reference materials (invite some of your students to help you find and organize them):

- Comprehensive atlases that provide details about the ocean
- Videotapes of programs about the ocean, such as those from ITV (Instructional Television) or the Discovery Channel
- Videotapes of news programs like "60 Minutes" to give students ideas for their presentations
- A listing of other TV programs about the ocean that will be aired in the next few days in your locale
- Names and addresses of local organizations and resource people—for example, the nearest aquarium; family members or neighbors whose jobs touch on the study or use of the ocean or of the living things in it; local authors or artists whose work portrays the sea

2. On the chalkboard or on poster paper list the ocean uses the students identified in Step 2.

Leave room after each for the class's definition of the term as derived from a general dictionary. Additional terms you may want to include are <u>fishing</u>, <u>energy</u>, <u>mining</u>, <u>transportation</u>, <u>desalination</u>, <u>recreation</u>, <u>ocean products</u>, and <u>food</u>. Ask students to refer to and discuss the list they brainstormed in Step 1 to predict which headlines stress concerns that scientists in each of these fields would have.

3. Ask students to work in cooperative learning groups of three or four students to concentrate on gathering information on one of the human uses of the ocean. Brainstorm with the class types of information to include in their report. Place this list where students can refer to and add to it throughout their investigation. Go over the questions reporters address in news reports: who, what, when, where, why, how. Distribute Activity Sheet 16 and ask groups or partner-teams to use the research materials you've provided to complete their news show outline. Explain that students should find as much concrete information as possible so that they can present their findings as a panel, clearly and persuasively, on the news show.

4. Show students a video of a news show or have students watch a show at home and take notes. Discuss the ways the reporters present their facts and make their reports interesting and visually appealing. Also discuss effective speaking techniques: maintaining good eye contact, being well prepared, and speaking loudly and clearly. Work with students to develop the criteria to evaluate the student news shows.

5. If you have access to a camcorder, decide if you or students will operate it. Either way, results will be much better if the camcorder is anchored to a tripod or resting on a desk. If students will operate the camcorder, instruct them in its proper use.

Conclusion:
1. Create a schedule for presentations and/or videotaping sessions for the news show. Have the other students watch and take notes on the presentations. Encourage students to give positive feedback to the groups presenting. If you make a videotape of the presentations, students may enjoy presenting it to other classes.

2. Encourage students to compare and contrast the different ways humans use the ocean to meet their needs.

3. Ask the class to develop a working statement about the possible conflicts involved in trying to use the ocean without abusing it. Students can add the class statement to the initial problem question in their individual portfolios.

STEP 4:
Focusing on Humans and Their Effects on Ocean Animals

Have students form the cooperative learning groups they will work in throughout this unit (you can maintain the same groups formed for the student news shows or expand group size if appropriate). Explain that each group will become expert on a particular human use of the ocean and how the related technology affects the ocean ecosystems.

Each group will use all eight *Zoobooks* in this module along with other research materials to find data about the effects of human use and technology on the ocean ecosystems. Before groups begin their research, use some of the *Zoobooks* to review study strategies with the class. Remind students to

- <u>Skim</u> the pictures and paragraphs to find (1) those that deal with what ocean animals need to maintain their health and populations; (2) those that show how ocean animals react to human use of the ocean.

- <u>Study</u> the pictures and paragraphs they've picked out to find details.

- <u>Compare</u> the *Zoobooks* data with information from other sources. Note areas of agreement. Write questions about facts that may seem to conflict, and why they may do so (e.g., When were facts noted? Where were they noted?, etc.).

- <u>Organize</u> their data using an easy reference system, such as a chart or a list. Note the source of their data, e.g., *Whales Zoobook*.

Distribute Activity Sheet 17 to all students. Make extra copies of this worksheet for groups to fill in during their culminating discussion, to use for their class presentations, and to add to their individual

83

portfolios to use again in Lesson 2. Explain that each individual group is to choose one of the uses of the ocean listed for Step 3. Then partner-teams within the group can research and—in pencil—note data to use in the columns on the worksheet. Remind partners to note sources of their data. Suggest that on the back of the worksheet they write references to pictures and diagrams that show how particular technological devices work.

The individual learning groups then reassemble to discuss and compare their worksheets and decide on which data to note on the final version they will present to the class. Two group members can be in charge of this transcription. Two or three members can draw pictures and diagrams to highlight key points on the sheet. Then the group can choose a member to present the final product to the class. Display the sheets and visuals and invite the class to study them to find out which of their questions from Lesson Step 1 and their predictions from Lesson Step 2 are represented.

partners, or by the cooperative learning groups. Suggest some examples of unit projects: a school- or community-wide education campaign about human dependence on the ocean; a portfolio of students' specific queries to regional and national organizations involved with use of the ocean, and with responses from these organizations; a student-made "special issue" *Zoobook* focusing on the impact of technology on several of the animals in the eight *Zoobooks* in this module; a cutaway diagram showing effects of human technological uses of the ocean. Students can also build some of this lesson's Curriculum Connections activities into unit projects.

List unit project ideas on the chalkboard, invite individuals or groups to choose one of them, and suggest that they begin their projects by listing steps, making assignments, developing evaluation criteria, and collecting materials they will need.

STEP 5:

Choosing a Unit Project

Explain that each student will be responsible for a unit project that shows how humans are interdependent parts of the ocean ecosystems. These projects can be done by individuals, by

ECOCONNECTION ACTIVITY

Encourage students to identify ways they interact with their mini-ecosystem. Then challenge them to list ways their interaction may affect the ecosystem.

EXPLORING OCEAN ECOSYSTEMS

CURRICULUM CONNECTIONS

Literature:
The Ocean in Mythology

Invite students to make a study of mythology that deals with the ocean—its creation, the animals that live in it, its power, its value, and the mythological heroes and heroines who have explored it. In the library, students can find ocean legends and myths in single-story volumes and in collections. Encourage them to find and read myths from several different cultures and to make a chart showing their likenesses and differences. As ways of sharing the myths with classmates, students can tell the stories aloud, act them out, rewrite and illustrate them for an anthology, or make a mural showing key events in myths of different cultures.

Creative Writing:
Ocean Myths for Today

Follow up the mythology activity by inviting students to write a mythic story about the ocean, set in modern times. As a pre-writing strategy, discuss the themes and attitudes that permeate ocean myths from most cultures, for example, the theme of human dependence on the ocean and attitudes of responsibility and stewardship. After writers share their original myths with a group of classmates, suggest that they add the myths to their individual portfolios and make copies for an anthology to use in your Reading Center.

Civics:
Attitude Surveys

Invite student teams to write and implement a survey to find out about attitudes toward the ocean held by students in other classrooms or by family members or other people in the community. Explain that the purpose of the survey is to gather information for an Ocean Education campaign. Suggest the following as a possible form for the survey: Make statements of 10 to 15 facts about the ocean, and ask the respondent to rate the importance of each on a scale from 1 to 5.

Example:
How important to you is each piece of information? Circle **5** for "very important," **4** for "important," **3** for "undecided," **2** for "somewhat unimportant," and **1** for "not important to me at all."

1. Ocean temperatures rise very slightly each year.   1   2   3   4   5
2. Many animals are trapped in fishing-fleet nets.   1   2   3   4   5

Stress the following to your survey designers:

- Each item is to state a fact, not the surveyor's opinion.
- Surveyors should choose facts they think are significant, based on their own study of the ocean and human dependence on it.
- Facts should be simply stated.

Surveyors can plan and assign the steps involved to classmates, such as writing the survey and copying the forms; distributing and explaining the survey and collecting the completed forms; tabulating the results on a master sheet; identifying the major areas that

indicate public knowledge or lack of knowledge, interest, concern, or awareness about human dependence on the ocean. Surveyors can then brainstorm for possible ways to upgrade general public knowledge about human interaction with the ocean.

As an evaluation strategy, discuss with the class how and why attitudes and knowledge about the ocean may vary. Ask students to give their reasons for why people may have differing attitudes and knowledge about the ocean—for example, differences in location, profession, interest, hobbies, education, etc. Each student or student group can create a poster designed to increase awareness, concern, or knowledge about a topic related to their survey results. If possible, have students conduct an Ocean Education campaign by displaying their posters at school or in the community.

Research Skills:
Using Periodicals

Suggest that a group of students keep a two- or three-week file of newspaper and news magazine articles that relate to human dependence on the ocean. Suggest that students write a label for each article identifying the major category or categories it falls into according to the terms listed in Step 3. Provide bulletin-board space, headed "Ocean Update," for students to post the latest articles. Encourage the class to refer to these postings to get current information for their unit projects or individual portfolios.

STUDENT PORTFOLIOS

Portfolios provide a way for students to organize the materials they develop in this unit and to assess their own progress. For this unit, have students create a portfolio titled Human Interaction with the Ocean. Portfolio enclosures from this lesson might include (1) the student's pre-assessment Idea Web; (2) the student's initial list of questions about human dependence on the ocean; (3) the student's copy of the question in "A PROBLEM TO SOLVE," with predictions about how ocean technology affects the ocean ecosystems; (4) the student's copies of Activity Sheets 16 and 17; (5) other materials resulting from the cooperative learning activity and from Curriculum Connection activities.

Preparing for the next lesson

On the chalkboard, write this statement: "*Everything depends upon everything else.*" Invite students to discuss this statement as it relates to what they have discovered so far about human interdependence with the ocean. Then invite students to make individual responses to the statement. Encourage a range of responses, such as poems, expository paragraphs, dialogues, paintings, idea webs, and picture panels. Students may wish to include their responses in a class display or put them into their portfolios.

ACTIVITY SHEET

16

Human Uses of the Ocean
NEWS SHOW OUTLINE

The ocean use my group has chosen for our news show is: _____

This use meets the following human needs: _____

_____

Important facts for our news show:

1. Who _____

2. What _____

3. When _____

4. Where _____

5. Why _____

6. How _____

Sources we used to find the information: _____

_____

_____

_____

_____

_____

These are the visuals (posters, clothing, other props) we will use to make our show more interesting: _____

_____

_____

(Use a separate sheet to write the script for your news show.)

87

ACTIVITY SHEET

17

HUMAN IMPACT ON THE OCEAN ECOSYSTEMS

My group is investigating this use of the ocean: _____

88

Use the space provided to describe possible impacts on the ocean ecosystems.

Possible *Positive* Impacts on:

1. Ocean Animals	
2. Ocean Plants	
3. Nonliving Parts of the Ocean	
4. Other Humans	

89

Possible *Negative* Impacts on:

1. Ocean Animals	
2. Ocean Plants	
3. Nonliving Parts of the Ocean	
4. Other Humans	

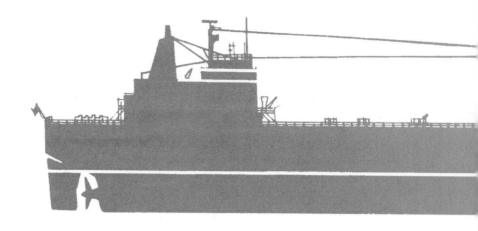

LESSON

2

AFFECTING THE OCEAN

Our interaction with ocean ecosystems affects the living and nonliving parts of the ocean.

INTRODUCTION

Students begin by brainstorming natural and human-caused disasters that affect the ocean ecosystems. Students then define "oil spill" and discuss how oil spills are cleaned up and what dangers oil spills present in the ocean. Students simulate an oil spill and investigate the effectiveness of different methods of cleaning up a spill. They then work in cooperative learning groups to investigate other human activities that may pose dangers to the ocean ecosystems. Finally, students continue to work on their unit projects.

OBJECTIVES:

1. To investigate methods of cleaning up an oil spill
2. To determine negative impacts of human use on the ocean ecosystems

YOU NEED:

1. Copies of the eight *Zoobooks* in this module
2. Back issues or clips from Spring 1989 news magazine reports on the Exxon Valdez oil spill and 1991 reports on the Persian Gulf spill

3. For the science investigation:
   - For each student, two copies of Activity Sheet 18
   - For each group, large white basin or plastic container; large measuring cup (at least 3 cups); water; handful of twigs and 1 foot of string to make a boom for containment; 1/4 cup to 1 cup of cooking oil; 1/2 cup liquid detergent; sponges or cotton balls; handful of straw (not hay); soda straws; aquarium net or nylon like that in stockings; dirt or sand; kaolin (diatomaceous earth); pieces of styrofoam; paper towels; carton or can for disposing of oil; blue food coloring to color water

Special Note:
This activity can be messy. To reduce the mess and the risk that students could damage their clothes, ask them to wear paint shirts, lab aprons, or some other protective clothing. Also, it is advisable to perform the procedure at lunch tables or some other area where spills can be easily washed away.

4. Research materials listed in Unit 3, Lesson 1, Step 3.

LESSON OUTLINE

Before the lesson begins:

1. Collect the materials needed for the oil spill.
2. Obtain articles on the Valdez or Persian Gulf oil spills or substitute another source: video, filmstrip, news article from a newspaper.
3. Duplicate Activity Sheet 18, two for each student.
4. Try the oil spill activity yourself so you know what to expect as students do the activity.

EXPLORING OCEAN ECOSYSTEMS

During the lesson:

1. Follow the lesson steps to have students

   (a) Brainstorm for prior knowledge of natural and human-caused ocean disasters.

   (b) Define the term OIL SPILL.

   (c) Perform the oil spill simulation.

   (d) Work in cooperative learning groups to investigate other potentially negative human impacts on the environment and ways to reduce risk to the environment.

   (e) Continue working on unit projects.

2. Have students continue writing in their Ocean Journals.

3. Have students continue to place completed work in their portfolios.

4. Direct students to continue to collect materials from magazines, newspapers, and other reading sources that give information about human uses of and impacts upon ocean ecosystems.

5. Words to add to your **Classroom Glossary**:

   Oil spill
   Disaster
   Tar balls
   Microscopic
   Crude oil
   Toxins
   Hydrocarbons
   Skimming
   Coagulate
   Dispersants

91

STEP 1:

Brainstorming for Prior Knowledge

Write NATURAL DISASTERS on the chalkboard. Ask students to brainstorm naturally occurring disasters that have negative impacts on the ocean ecosystems. Next, write HUMAN-CAUSED DISASTERS on the board. Elicit from students disasters they have heard about (oil spills, pollution, etc.) that are caused by humans.

STEP 2:

Defining Terms: <u>Oil Spill</u>

Ahead of time, invite interested students to skim the articles (see 2 under "YOU NEED" and "Before the lesson begins") to find out when and where the oil spills happened and what immediate problems developed. Invite these students to share the data with the class. Then amplify the data with the following background information, and pose the brainstorming questions at the end of each paragraph.

What is Oil? Oil is a hydrocarbon (a naturally occurring compound of hydrogen and carbon). It forms when buried remains of plants and animals "cook" at moderate temperatures and pressures deep in the Earth's crust. Crude oil comes directly from the ground, and already contains some toxic hydrocarbons, like benzene. We refine oil by separating it into various products, like heating oil and gasoline. <u>BRAINSTORM</u>: How do we depend on refined oil?

What happens when oil mixes with water? First, it forms a smelly, gloppy substance called "chocolate mousse." This floating mousse is called a "pancake," and it immediately starts to spread. Then, as water and lighter parts of the crude oil evaporate, the pancake thickens and hardens, forming "tar balls." Eventually, these tar balls will sink. <u>BRAINSTORM</u>: Think up or predict some ways we might clean up (1) the pancake; (2) the tar balls.

How do we try to clean up oil spills? Is it easy to do? Cleanup methods depend on the type of oil spilled and the conditions of the water where it

was spilled, but usually several methods are used on one spill. The methods are directed toward absorbing the oil, or containing and skimming it off while it floats, or catching it as it coagulates and sinks. While the spilled oil is still a pancake, we try to clean it up with dispersants—chemicals like detergents—which break the oil down into tiny pieces. At the same time, workers go out with booms—floating "sausages" with skirts that hang a few feet below the surface—in an attempt to corral the floating oil. Then skimmers come along to collect this oil by scooping or sucking it up. As for tar balls, these have to be picked up by hand before they sink. All in all, the oil is extremely difficult to remove. An authority at the National Oceanic and Atmospheric Administration estimates that all these cleanup efforts combined can get rid of only about 10% of spilled oil. <u>BRAINSTORM</u>: Predict some ways in which oil spills affect living things in the ocean ecosystems.

What dangers do oil spills cause in the ocean ecosystems? When the tar balls sink, they destroy microbes and other living things. Fish and microscopic animals and plants at the base of the food chain absorb the oil in their food, thus poisoning their systems and the systems of animals that eat them. Seabirds either freeze when their feathers become coated and clumped together by oil, or they drown because their buoyancy is reduced by the oil on their bodies. Nesting birds that bring even one drop of oil back on their bodies when they return to the nest can destroy their eggs. (Oil coats the egg and does not allow oxygen to get through.) Oil clumps together the hair or fur of sea mammals, like otters, so that icy water reaches their skin and they freeze; or the otters ingest large doses of toxic compounds when they clean their fur and die from organ damage as the toxins invade their bodies. <u>BRAINSTORM</u>: Should we care about how oil spills affect the ocean ecosystems? Why or why not? (Since this question directly relates to the "PROBLEM TO SOLVE" for this unit [see page 82] write students' ideas and responses on the chalkboard or on oaktag for display and referral.)

Conclude the brainstorming session by reading the second lesson objective to students and inviting them to discuss and write questions they wish to explore further as they work through this lesson. Focus queries by suggesting that members of the cooperative learning groups formed in Lesson 1 pose questions about how

92

the particular human use of the ocean that they are studying can cause pollution or another potential disaster to the ocean.

STEP 3:

Investigation:
Getting Oil out of the Water

Estimated time:1-2 class periods

This investigation provides an opportunity for students to find out firsthand the difficulties in cleaning up an oil spill and to devise, compare, and contrast some methods for doing so.

Procedure:

1. Ahead of time, place in a central location the materials listed under "YOU NEED." Also give each student two copies of Activity Sheet 18 so two different cleanup methods can be recorded.

2. Divide the class up into teams. Explain that each team represents EPA (Environmental Protection Agency) workers rushing to the scene of a grounded tanker spilling oil into the ocean. Each team's task is to use the materials to devise one method for cleaning up the oil spill in calm water and then, if time permits, in rough water.

3. List and discuss the following methods and materials. Encourage each group to predict the effectiveness of its strategy as they choose it. You might also invite groups to devise other strategies of their own. Each team should use the same amount of water and oil in each trial so teams can compare the results.

   (a) straw: place on oil and remove

   (b) paper towel: place on oil and remove

   (c) styrofoam pieces: place on oil and remove

   (d) boom of twigs tied together and pulled around the spill to contain it

   (e) soda straw: blow bubbles under the oil to see if a ring of bubbles will contain the spill

   (f) detergent: add a drop to the spill to disperse the oil

   (g) sand sprinkled on the surface of the oily water

   (h) kaolin sprinkled on the oily water

   (i) aquarium net or nylon as a scoop for the oil

As students choose their method, have them write in the materials they're using on Activity Sheet 18.

4. Give each team a basin or plastic container of water, a large measuring cup filled with 2 cups of dyed-blue water, and 1/4 cup of oil. Instruct them to place the measuring cup inside the basin to contain any spills, add the 1/4 cup of oil to the 2 cups of water to create their own "spill," and then use their first chosen method to try to clean up the spill in calm water. After students have tried the first method, have them add water to the measuring cup so that the water is again at the 2-cup level. Have students read and record the amount of oil left in the cup. (The cup will contain some water and a floating layer of oil.)

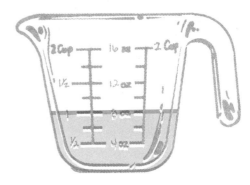

This represents the amount of oil that was not cleaned up.

Next, to create a second, identical oil spill, have students add more oil to the measuring cup so that it reads 2 cups of water and 1/4 cup of oil.

Then have students repeat the cleanup using the same method in rough water. To simulate rough water, one student can gently blow over the water with a drinking straw while teammates continue trying to clean up the spill. Remind students to note on their Activity Sheets the effectiveness of their first method in both calm and rough water.

Now have students repeat each step in this investigation using the second method they chose to contain their oil spills. Tell them to use a clean copy of Activity Sheet 18. This way they can compare the effectiveness of two different containment methods.

93

When everyone is finished, have each team share its results. Discuss which method was most effective. (The most effective method will leave the least amount of oil in the measuring cup). Emphasize that the effectiveness of either of the methods chosen may change depending upon whether ocean waters are calm or rough.

Teams can conclude their investigations by writing their EPA report to recommend the better of their two ways for cleaning up the oil spill, giving reasons for their choice. Reports should include data from their Activity Sheets and any comments and recommendations about a procedure that works better in calm or rough water.

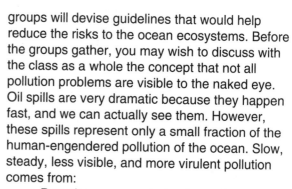

Conclusion:

Based on their own experiences within their team and their own insights, ask students to respond to the following discussion questions:

1. Which materials clean up oil by absorbing it? Which ones work best?

2. What did detergents do to the oil spill?

3. How can workers prevent an oil spill from spreading? That is, which materials worked best for containing the oil?

4. How did rough water affect different cleanup efforts?

5. Would the same method work best for every oil spill? Why or why not?

6. How might oil spills be prevented?

7. The investigations you've done deal only with cleaning up oil in the water. What techniques could you use to clean up oil when it reaches the beaches?

STEP 4:

Focusing on Negative Impacts of Human Uses of the Ocean

Students will return to the cooperative learning groups they organized in Lesson 1 to explore in more detail any negative impacts human uses of the ocean have on ocean ecosystems. Then

groups will devise guidelines that would help reduce the risks to the ocean ecosystems. Before the groups gather, you may wish to discuss with the class as a whole the concept that not all pollution problems are visible to the naked eye. Oil spills are very dramatic because they happen fast, and we can actually see them. However, these spills represent only a small fraction of the human-engendered pollution of the ocean. Slow, steady, less visible, and more virulent pollution comes from:

- Dumping sewage sludge (organic, industrial, and human refuse) in the ocean.

- Dumping garbage containing nonbiodegradable materials (plastics, glass, aluminum) into the ocean.

- Agricultural runoff, made of pesticides and herbicides, working its way through water systems (rivers) and food chains until it reaches its calamitous peak in the ocean.

- Municipal and industrial drainage systems, contaminated with oil, toxic chemicals, and heavy metals that work their way into the sediment of river beds and then into the ocean.

- Nuclear reactors, causing thermal pollution by dumping warm water into coastal waters, which increases the temperature of the ocean water. This may harm some ocean life adapted to cooler temperatures.

- Oil refineries—usually along coasts—whose accidental seepage poisons salt marshes and estuaries that people depend on as a source of food.

After the class has discussed these and any other possible sources of pollution in their own area, ask your cooperative learning groups to do further research.

Students should focus on the negative impacts of the Human Impact on the Ocean Ecosystems that were listed on Activity Sheet 17 in the previous lesson and on how this human use negatively impacts the ocean ecosystems. Students would then brainstorm ideas to form guidelines that would help reduce the negative impacts on the ocean environment. The *Zoobooks* in this module will make a good research spin-off point. One group member can summarize the group's decision on the chart. Provide time for a spokesperson appointed by the group to present findings to the class. Students can also write to both environmental groups and industry groups responsible for this human use (nuclear power plants, oil companies) to ask what guidelines they suggest for protecting the ocean and for additional information on how each group's use affects the ocean.

STEP 5:
Continuing the Unit Projects

Remind students that the purpose of their unit projects is to show how humans are dependent upon the ocean ecosystems. Challenge them to find ways—in words or pictures—to show how human use impacts the ocean. For example, students who are doing cutaway diagrams of technological devices for mining and for extracting oil might add symbols, pictures, or labels to identify resultant pollutants or other dangers to ocean life.

ECOCONNECTION ACTIVITY

Have a student call a local pet store or read a book on aquarium or terrarium care to identify possible environmental hazards to aquariums (for example, spraying cleaners near an aquarium). Discuss with students ways to prevent harm to the aquarium or terrarium. Observe your mini-ecosystem to identify possible environmental hazards to its living things. Encourage students to brainstorm possible solutions.

CURRICULUM CONNECTIONS

Math:
Track Your Trash

Ask each student to bring a bag to school in which each will place all of the trash he or she creates in one day. Instead of throwing trash in the trash can, all paper, aluminum, glass, and other items will go into the bag. If students throw away anything organic (fruit, vegetables, other food products), they should estimate the amount thrown away (1/4, 1/2, 1 cup) and write this on a piece of paper with a drawing of the item. They then throw the actual organic material in the trash can, but place the paper with their drawing and quantity estimation into their bag to record the food item. Tell students to take the bag home, continue to use it throughout the evening and next morning, and bring it back to class the next day. Distribute graph paper and have students create a graph of their trash. For example, students might select categories: plastic, paper, food, aluminum. Then have students count the number of each item accumulated.

Students can also sort their items into recyclable and nonrecyclable trash. Finally, students can use math skills to estimate the amount of trash they create in one week, one month, and one year. Additionally, students can combine their data to find out how much trash the class as a whole creates in one day, week, and year.

Social Studies:
Sources of Energy

Suggest that a group of students research sources of energy currently in use or being developed. These include oil, coal, natural gas, nuclear power, hydropower, solar power, tide and wave power from the ocean, wind, geothermal power, and biomass energy (plant—chiefly wood—or animal matter converted into fuel). Encourage the group to present its findings in the form of pictures or diagrams to illustrate each energy source. Suggest that captions for each illustration include the following basic data: (1) how it works; (2) where in the world that form

95

of energy is chiefly used now; (3) any negative impacts resulting from the energy technology. After the group presents its pictures and captions, display them and invite all your students to study them further to prepare for a discussion. Suggested discussion questions: (1) *"Which technologies are 'cleanest,' i.e., have the least negative impacts on the environment?"* (2) *"In your opinion, which technologies are under-used?"* (3) *"Which energy sources could be introduced into and used in your state or region?"*

Library Research:
Ocean Follow-Ups

Invite students to research the current status of an ocean animal and create their own revised, up-to-the minute *"Zoobook"* containing the latest information on that animal. Suggest students use *Zoobooks* and natural history maps to identify ocean animals directly affected by the Valdez or Persian Gulf oil spills, and then to find recent articles in newspapers and magazines that describe the ongoing effects of the spills, right up to the present time. To help your researchers get going, you or a librarian may wish to review with them the use of *The Reader's Guide to Periodical Literature, The Reader's Guide Abstracts,* and any computerized information retrieval system your library has, such as InfoTrac. After students collect their data, invite them to brainstorm different ways of organizing it, such as time lines, illustrated reports, or chalk-talks for the class. Some students may wish to make drawings or photocopies of *Zoobooks* animals affected by the spills, write new captions to describe the effects, and bind the pictures and captions into their newly created *"Zoobooks."*

Preparing for the next lesson

Ask students to continue building their Human Interaction with the Ocean Portfolios with materials developed in this lesson. As a review and organizational strategy, suggest that they make a draft of a portfolio Table of Contents, then determine which sections of their portfolios they would like to fill out with more information. Suggest that students confer with you or with a study partner to discuss their portfolios and the goals they have for completing them.

ACTIVITY SHEET

18

RECORDS AND RESULTS:
CLEANING UP AN OIL SPILL

Use this chart to record what happens as your group tries to clean up an oil spill. You will be given <u>two</u> copies of this chart so your group can try two different methods.

	Calm Water					Rough Water				
Materials Used										
Time to Clean Spill										
Amount of Oil Not Cleaned Up										
Rate of Effectiveness— use a scale of 1 to 5 (5 = most effective)	1	2	3	4	5	1	2	3	4	5

Was the cleanup more effective in calm or rough water? _____

How would you change your method to make it work better?_____

Conclusions: _____

_____

_____

LESSON 3

ASSUMING RESPONSIBILITY FOR THE OCEAN ECOSYSTEMS

We have the responsibility to ensure that our actions do not harm the ocean ecosystems.

INTRODUCTION

Students begin exploring the concept of responsibility for the ocean ecosystems by discussing who should be responsible for cleaning up an oil spill. Students then define the term "responsible." Students are challenged to consider the differences between legal and ethical responsibility. Next, students participate in a simulation in which they become residents of a town whose City Council must decide whether or not to build on an area of land used by least terns for nesting. Students then return to their cooperative learning groups to consider how the human use of the ocean they are investigating affects ocean ecosystems. Finally, students complete their unit projects.

OBJECTIVES:

1. To explore issues of responsibility and concern
2. To explore ways of interacting positively with the ocean ecosystems

YOU NEED:

1. Copies of the eight *Zoobooks* in this module
2. "City Council Meeting" Activity Sheets
3. To make the City Council Meeting simulation more realistic, obtain a videotape of a council meeting or ask a city official to talk to the class about a meeting.
4. Ahead of time, for Step 4, arrange for one or both of the following:

   • Show a videotape of an oceanographer or ocean animal biologist at work. Ask your reference librarian for help. Readily obtainable are videotapes of the work of Jacques Cousteau and Dr. Louis M. Herman.

   • Invite a guest speaker involved with conservation, animal husbandry, or an ecological or environmental organization to discuss her or his work with the class. Invite another speaker involved with developing an ocean technology to talk to the class, too. As a guide for your guests, explain to them ahead of time what the objectives of this lesson are (see 1 and 2 at left).

5. Copies of Activity Sheet 19
6. Oaktag, markers, crayons, and other art materials

LESSON OUTLINE

Before the lesson begins:

1. Collect the art materials listed above.
2. Obtain videotapes and/or speakers for Steps 3 and 4.
3. Decide upon roles for each student in the City Council Meeting simulation.
4. Duplicate the appropriate number of copies for each sheet needed in the simulation (see page 105 at the end of this unit)
5. Duplicate Activity Sheet 19 for Step 4, two copies for each student.
6. Provide *Zoobooks* for use in Step 4 and Curriculum Connections activities.

During the Lesson:

1. Follow the lesson steps to have students

   (a) Brainstorm for prior knowledge of responsibility.

   (b) Define the term RESPONSIBLE.

   (c) Follow the procedures for the City Council Meeting simulation.

   (d) Break up into cooperative learning groups and have students complete Activity Sheet 19 to find ways people can use the ocean responsibly.

   (e) Conclude their unit projects.

2. Direct students to continue their Ocean Journals.

3. Have students evaluate their portfolios.

4. Words to add to your **Classroom Glossary**:

   Responsibility
   Legal
   Ethical

STEP 1:

Brainstorming for Prior Knowledge

Invite students to briefly review the major impressions they got from studying the Exxon Valdez oil spill (Unit 3, Lesson 2). Then, to introduce the concept of responsibility, ask the class: *"Who should be responsible for cleaning up an oil spill?"* (DON'T expect or invite closure in this activity. DO invite debate and discussion.) Call on volunteers to suggest why responsibility might be laid to the captain of the ship; the pilot (the expert on local waters who advises the captain about navigating through them); the oil company that owns the ship; the company that built the ship; the people who live in the area of the spill; the EPA; people from many places who are concerned about the ocean ecosystems; oil company customers; any other individuals or groups the students suggest. Ask students to make a "because" statement part of their response (e.g., "I think the shipbuilder is responsible, because...."). Write "because" statements on the chalkboard or on poster paper to refer to throughout the lesson (e.g., "...because companies that build oil tankers should make the hulls strong enough not to break in collisions"). Wind up the brainstorming session by inviting students to share any questions that occur to them now about responsibility.

STEP 2:

Defining Terms: Responsible

As you know, "responsibility" is a hot topic because it is inevitably linked to another hot topic, "values." An objective way to move into the consideration of responsibility is to rely on the dictionary. Invite volunteers to look up dictionary definitions of responsible and share them with the class. Most of these definitions involve (1) being obliged or expected to do something (this involves legal or ethical accountability for the care and welfare of ourselves and others); (2) deserving credit or blame; (3) being trustworthy or reliable.

Then invite students to discuss which definition is illustrated in each of the following sentences and to create other sample sentences:

(a) Traffic laws say school bus drivers have the <u>responsibility</u> to drive within a certain speed limit (<u>legal</u> responsibility). Teachers and parents say children have the <u>responsibility</u> for turning in schoolwork that represents their own efforts (<u>ethical</u> responsibility).

(b) Our group is <u>responsible</u> for this wonderful mural. My brother is <u>responsible</u> for spilling paint on the floor.

(c) We know she's a <u>responsible</u> person, because she kept her promise about bringing a chart to school.

Finally, focus again on the first definition and examples. Discuss how <u>legal</u> responsibilities are usually clear because they are written down (codified) and the penalties stated, while <u>ethical</u> responsibilities are not always so clear, because people often disagree about what they are. Pave the way for Step 3 by explaining that groups of people often disagree about what their ethical responsibilities are toward ensuring that human actions do not harm the ocean ecosystems.

STEP 3:

Investigation: Simulating a City Council Meeting

Estimated time: 3-5 class periods

This simulation enables students to (1) act out and thus better understand the often-competing concerns of different groups who rely in one way or another on the ocean ecosystems; (2) clarify and analyze their own values concerning the ocean ecosystems so that they can take appropriate actions based upon their beliefs. You may first wish to discuss with your class how all living things—including humans—are concerned with basic survival needs: food, water, space, shelter, air; and how a growing population of humans puts extraordinary demands on the Earth to meet those needs. Depending upon the maturity of your students, you might include a discussion of the difference between satisfying immediate needs and providing for the future.

Procedure:
Below is a five-day guide to follow for the simulation.

DAY 1

1. Explain to students that they will be participating in a simulation to help them learn how people work together to solve real-life problems, and that usually there are no clear answers to these problems. Tell students that each one will be assigned a role to play in the simulation and that on the last two days of the simulation, all will participate in a "City Council Meeting."

2. Distribute the City Council Information Sheet. Read and discuss with the students. If possible, show a video of a City Council meeting or have a council member present to answer questions.

3. Distribute, read, and discuss the Project Description, Least Tern Information Sheet, and Environmental Impact Report.

DAY 2

1. Review the simulation and answer questions.

2. Assign students to the following groups and distribute role cards and worksheets. (**Note:** Divide up roles so there are an equal number of students who are for and against the issue.)

Council Members ....**ALL NEUTRAL**
    1 Council President
    1 Council Secretary (the City Clerk)
    1 Council Sergeant at Arms
    4-6 Council Members

City Officials ....**ALL NEUTRAL**
    1 City Planner
    1 Environmental Planner

1-3 Reporters....................................**NEUTRAL**

1 Landowner ....**FOR**

1 Builder..**FOR**

4 Business Owners..................................**FOR**

3 Construction Worker
    Association Members ....**FOR**

4 Homeowners ....AGAINST

2 Bird Watchers Society Members...AGAINST

3 Fishing Association Members ....AGAINST

2 PTA Parents.................................AGAINST

3. Assign or have students elect the following cooperative learning roles (for the last eight groups presenting their positions at the meeting):

Speaker: speaks at the council meeting
Reader: reads handouts
Writer: writes down the groups' ideas
Artist: draws a picture of the groups' project presentation

4. Instruct groups who will be making a presentation at the City Council Meeting to read the Project Description, discuss their position, and then write a speech and make a drawing of their proposal for the meeting.

5. Meet with the City Council officials to go over the City Council Meeting Agenda and Council Worksheet.

6. Meet with the reporters and discuss how to conduct an interview and write an article.

DAY 3

1. Review and discuss simulation questions with students.

2. Assist individual groups as needed.

DAYS 4-5

1. Begin the simulation following the Council Meeting Agenda after distributing a copy to students. Continue on the second day if needed.

2. After the Council has voted, allow students to discuss the results and evaluate the simulation.

Evaluation:
After the City Council presents its conclusion, invite students to respond to the following questions either in writing or orally:

1. Are you satisfied with the City Council's recommendation? Why or why not?

2. If your group's recommendation were taken, how would it affect (a) your group; (b) the other groups; (c) the lagoon and related ocean ecosystem?

3. In the Council Meeting, what did you learn about conflicts that arise when humans interact with the ocean ecosystems?

4. As you worked in your group, what were your responsibilities toward the welfare of people in that group? What, if any, did you feel your responsibilities toward the ocean ecosystem to be?

5. What's the difference between long-range goals and immediate goals? Did your group represent one or both? Explain.

6. Does your group depend on the long-range health of the ocean ecosystems? Explain.

7. Have you changed your mind in any way about your group's position? Tell why or why not.

8. Apply what you've learned to an environmental situation or problem in your community or state.

STEP 4:
Looking for Responsible Solutions

Students will return to their cooperative learning groups to explore ways in which humans can use the ocean's resources responsibly. Students should look for ways to ensure the well-being of the ocean ecosystems while still meeting long-range human demands. Each group will produce an illustrated Idea Web to display for the class.

Begin with a presentation to the whole class of the video and/or speakers suggested under "YOU NEED." Suggest that your student audience listen and look to identify ways in which (1) humans interact negatively with an ecosystem; (2) humans interact positively with it; (3) negative impacts might be lessened or done away with entirely.

Distribute Activity Sheet 19. In each group, members can work together—on the basis of what they've learned in previous lessons—to note facts for the first circle in the web. Ask groups to list these facts. Then suggest that the group members pair off. Each partner-team chooses a fact from the circle and gathers data that could be presented in circles 2 and 3: a negative impact of the technology on an ocean ecosystem, and an immediate or long-range result of that impact on humans. As an example, you might discuss "improved" technologies for drilling for oil in the ocean: an immediate benefit for humans is more

101

energy. A negative impact on an ocean ecosystem is the killing of whole species of fish. In turn, a negative impact on humans is less fish to eat.

After partners have made their notes for circles 2 and 3, they use reference materials to find suggestions from scientists about how to avoid the negative impact on the ocean ecosystems and, in turn, on humans. At this point, encourage students to talk to representatives of other groups as part of their research. For example, partners in the fishing group might confer with the groups involved with desalination, mining, or energy to find out how the different technologies harm the ocean ecosystems and what strategies, if any, those technologies use to safeguard ocean animals.

When individual group members reassemble, members can work as a group to share their discoveries and insights and to write concise statements on a clean copy of Activity Sheet 19. Then each group can assign members to make large copies on oaktag of each Idea Web circle

and illustrate a major concept in that circle. Refer students to the *Zoobooks* for ideas for pictures, graphs, charts, and other illustrative devices. Display the big webs in a central area for the class to study as spokespersons from the different groups present and explain them. Keep the webs on display for students to use during Unit Wind-Up and Assessment.

STEP 5:
Finalizing the Unit Projects

Remind students to include in their projects their own ideas about human responsibility for the ocean ecosystems. Suggest that as they complete their projects they make sure to include data not only about how humans use ocean ecosystems, but also about why humans need healthy ocean ecosystems.

ECOCONNECTION ACTIVITY

Ask students what responsibilities they have in caring for the aquarium, terrarium, or mini-ecosystem.

CURRICULUM CONNECTIONS
Social Studies/Civics

Discuss why environmental concerns and programs can best be implemented by people working together in groups. As a discussion prompt, ask what the observable difference is between one person recycling or picking up litter and a group of people organizing to do the same tasks. Invite students to devise group strategies for implementing better methods for protecting the ocean ecosystems. Examples are letter-writing campaigns to elected representatives in local, state, and federal government; community education through posters and rallies; letters to the editors of local newspapers; boycotts of companies selling products that result from harming the ocean ecosystems; "update" meetings to keep themselves and others informed about new and immediate threats to the environment.

Encourage your class to organize into groups to act on ocean ecosystem threats, using some of the strategies discussed. To stress the reality of empowerment, remind your class that it was because of the written and oral protests of thousands of students that United States tuna fishers and canners have tried to devise methods of catching tuna without trapping and killing dolphins, and that moratoriums on whale hunts have been greatly influenced by thousands of students all around the world who wrote to officials of whaling nations and asked them to amend or stop the whale-kill.

Health:
What's in It for Me?

Invite partners or small groups to investigate the relationship between substances that are harmful to humans and substances that are harmful to animals in the ocean ecosystems. Challenge these students to find examples of chemicals, agricultural and municipal runoffs, sewage-sludge dumping, and nuclear reactor cooling water that eventually affect human health as well as the health of ocean life. Ask students to focus on the biological reasons why all living things—including human beings—are eventually affected by pollutants.

Literature:
Small Deeds

While there are many new books for young people that directly stress environmental concerns (such as Dr. Seuss's *The Lorax*), there are also many "golden oldies" that show individual characters interacting in positive and "do-able" ways with the environment. For example, in Barbara Cooney's *Miss Rumphius*, the main character finds a simple way to make the world more beautiful. In Patricia MacLachlan's *Sarah, Plain and Tall*, the title character imbues her

young charges with an awe and respect for the sea and the animals in it. In *Hawk, I'm Your Brother*, Byrd Baylor wraps a gripping story around the concept of the likenesses and differences between a wild bird and its loving keeper. In her *Thirteen Moon* books, Jean Craighead George points out, without preaching, the delicate balances that enable animals to live from season to season. Make these books available to your students and ask them to find others, both fiction and nonfiction, that show humans involved in a positive way with their natural environments. Invite reading partners to explore one of the books together and then report to the class about how the author or main human character shows feelings of responsibility toward the environment and about how the students and their classmates might emulate the character's behavior in their own day-to-day lives.

Creative Writing:
One Hundred Years
from Now...

Invite interested students to work independently or with a partner to write a science fiction story based on the premise that within a century, human beings will have learned how to live in a positive way with the living things in the ocean, so that neither humans nor ocean animals are threatened. Encourage your writers to use data from this unit to provide details in their stories. Since all stories need a "villain" or a "problem," suggest that a villain might be someone who wishes to return to an "old" 20th century technology, or that a problem might be how to adapt technology to an ever-growing human population. Suggest that writers illustrate their stories for a classroom anthology, enact the stories "live" or on tape, or draw story picture panels to display on a bulletin board.

Expository Writing:
Zoobooks 2100

Using the 100-years-from-now approach just described, invite students to choose a *Zoobook* from this module and "update" it, or pages from it, to show their predictions about the animal 100 years from now. Prompt questions to use: Will otters be extinct or will there be more of them? Will humans have learned how to communicate with dolphins? Will penguins have adapted to warmer ocean waters? Will humans have found a way to use plankton for their own food? If so, how will baleen whales be doing? Suggest that students make copies of *Zoobooks* illustrations and write new captions for them to tell about the 100-years-from-now state of the ocean. As your writers share their updated *"Zoobooks 2100"* with classmates, invite the audience to tell what they like best about the new magazines and to pose questions about the future-facts the authors have presented.

UNIT WIND-UP AND ASSESSMENT

1. Ask students to examine the Idea Web they created at the beginning of this unit (these webs should be in their portfolios). Then have them create a new, revised web based on what they've learned during this unit.

2. Ask small groups of students to review their unit findings to respond to the problem posed in Lesson 1: *"In what ways can humans use the ocean ecosystems without harming them?"* Bring the class together to discuss the groups' responses and combine these in a response almost all students agree to. Students should be able to use the class response to develop a three-column list:

(a) How humans use the ocean ecosystems

(b) How humans harm the ocean ecosystems

(c) Methods humans are exploring to use the ocean ecosystems without harming them

Invite students to apply their class response and their lists to another ecosystem with which they are familiar.

3. Schedule presentations of the unit projects. Beforehand, develop with the class a set of criteria that students will use when assessing their own and other unit projects. See the *Teaching Strategies* Supplement for criteria ideas.

4. Ask students to organize their portfolios for this unit. Allow time for them to complete or revise their materials. Ask each student to write an evaluation of her or his portfolio to tell about (a) what the student learned; (b) what ideas or concepts are most important to the student; (c) what the student would like to find out more about. Invite students to share and discuss their completed portfolios with you or with another partner to point out sections the student is proudest of, which goals have been met, and which goals remain.

PHOTOCOPYING INSTRUCTIONS
FOR THE SIMULATION

City Council Information Sheet:	*1 copy for each student*
Project Description:	*1 copy for each student*
Environmental Impact Report:	*1 copy for each student*
Least Tern Information Sheet:	*1 copy for each student*
City Council Group Worksheet:	*1 copy for every student in the City Council Group*
Council President Worksheet:	*1 copy for the Council President*
City Clerk Worksheet:	*1 copy for the City Clerk*
City Council Meeting Agenda:	*1 copy for the City Clerk, who fills in and returns to you to make 1 copy for each student*
Sergeant at Arms Worksheet:	*1 copy for the Sergeant at Arms*
"Request to Speak" Cards:	*2 copies for the Sergeant at Arms (who fills in the names of speakers representing the 8 groups making presentations at the meeting)*
Speaking Groups Planning Sheet:	*1 copy for every student in the 8 presentation groups*
Speaking Groups Role Cards:	*1 copy of the appropriate card for every student in the 8 presentation groups*
Reporters Worksheet:	*1 copy for each reporter*

105

Zoobooks®

CITY COUNCIL INFORMATION SHEET

The City Council is the legislative or law-making branch of the city government. The members of the Council make the laws that govern the city. There are up to 15 members on the City Council. Each Council member is elected for a four-year term. The members of the Council elect one of their members to be President of the Council.

The City Council has power to make decisions about the lives and property of its citizens. The City Council has the right to do the following:

- tax citizens

106

- take a citizen's property for public use (after paying for the property)

- tell citizens how and for what purposes they may use their own property

- regulate businesses in the city

- declare a citizen's conduct in violation of the law if the citizen does not follow the City Council's rulings.

City Council Meetings are open to the public. Citizens may ask questions and argue for or against a topic on the agenda. The public is given a specific amount of time to speak. After the Council has heard from both sides of the issue, it may make a decision.

After the City Council has made a ruling, the Mayor is responsible for seeing that the laws are carried out. The Mayor is part of the city's executive branch, just as the President is part of the nation's executive branch. The City Attorney is part of the judicial branch of the city government. The City Attorney explains laws to the citizens and prosecutes citizens who break the laws.

PROJECT DESCRIPTION

Written by the City Planner

The builder, _____, and landowner, _____, propose to build 50 new homes and a 100-room high-rise hotel around Clear Lagoon. The lots and homes will be small to make them affordable. The 10-story hotel will take up only a narrow portion of the shoreline and will have direct access to the park next to it.

The owner, _____, will donate a portion of the land to the city. This donated land will be developed into a park and recreation facility by the owner, _____, at no expense to the city. The recreation facility will include boat ramps, a public dock, a walking bridge to the island, and public restrooms. Beaches will also be added.

All beaches in front of the homes will remain public. This means that anyone may use these beaches. Each homeowner may construct a dock in front of his or her home. All homes will be landscaped.

Except for gasoline-powered boats, lake pollution will be kept to a minimum. An extensive drainage system will be installed to combat the erosion at the south end of the lake.

107

ENVIRONMENTAL IMPACT REPORT

Prepared by the Environmental Planner

Impact on the Environment

Once there were many least terns in this region, but their numbers have been decreasing. The tern lays and hatches its eggs on the beach. With the increase of building and recreation along the coast, the least tern has been unable to find nesting areas. The shore of Clear Lagoon is one of the few remaining areas along the coast where least terns can lay and hatch their eggs.

The least tern feeds on the fish from the lagoon. One of the proposed recreational uses of the lagoon is fishing. Until now, the owner of the lagoon has leased it to the Clear Lagoon Fishing Association. Association membership is about 50.

Because the dirt road is impassable in winter, fishing occurs only in the drier months. Building a road and making fishing available to anyone will seriously decrease the number of fish in the lagoon. Because of lack of fish, the least tern population may decrease even more.

There is severe erosion caused by a brushfire at the south end of the lake. The project's landscaping will stop this erosion.

108

Impact on the City

This project offers the city a much-needed recreational area. Gang activity, which is currently on the increase, should decrease if a park is provided where children can play.

The construction of the homes and the hotel will put many unemployed people to work. The construction of the development will create about 1,000 jobs. The hotel and surrounding businesses will employ about 50 people. Taxes from the new residents and the hotel will help the city, which is experiencing financial problems.

LEAST TERN INFORMATION SHEET

The least tern is a graceful water bird found along the coast. It has a sharp bill and a forked tail. With a length of 9 inches, it is the smallest of the terns. The least tern often hovers and plunges headfirst into the water to feed on small fish and insects. It nests on sandy beaches or gravel.

Humans' great use of the coastline and sandy beaches has led to the destruction of the least tern's nesting areas. Approximately 1,200 breeding pairs still exist. The least tern is classified as an endangered species and its numbers are decreasing.

CITY COUNCIL GROUP WORKSHEET

1. Elect the following officers:

    PRESIDENT presides at the City Council Meeting and votes.

    SERGEANT AT ARMS is the Police Officer who keeps order at the Council Meeting.

    CITY CLERK announces speakers, records Council members' votes.

    CITY COUNCIL MEMBERS listen to the Public Hearing, ask questions, vote.

2. Read the FOR and AGAINST List below. Then decide which of the FOR and AGAINST issues are most important to you. Write down questions you have for the City Planner, Environmental Planner, Builder, Landowner, and other groups. (**Note:** You should not decide how you will vote **until after you hear people speak** at the Council Meeting.)

    FOR and AGAINST List

    FOR

    - The project will <u>increase employment</u> in the city.
    - The city will <u>get more tax money</u> from the new businesses and homes, which will help the financially troubled city.
    - There will be more <u>affordable housing</u> for people in the city.
    - The project will build a <u>recreational facility</u> for the city for free.
    - <u>More tourists</u> will come to the city and spend money at local businesses.

    AGAINST

    - The least tern will <u>lose its nesting spot</u> in the area.
    - Much of the <u>natural beauty</u> of the shoreline will be destroyed.
    - There will be <u>more pollution</u> caused by motorboats and people in the area.
    - <u>Traffic will increase</u> on the road into the lagoon.
    - The homes overlooking the lagoon may <u>decrease in value</u>.
    - Waterfowl and other <u>wildlife will decrease</u> around the lagoon.

3. During the Council Meeting you will take notes and write down any questions you have. You may ask questions during the question period.

4. After the Public Hearing you will work with the other Council members to decide what to do about the project. You may choose to accept the project as it is, change the project, or reject the project.

5. You will vote "AYE" or "NAY" on the proposal.

QUESTIONS: _____

_____

_____

_____

_____

110

COUNCIL PRESIDENT WORKSHEET

You are the President of the City Council. It is your job to conduct the meeting and make sure the Council Meeting is run in an orderly and proper fashion.

As a member of the council you may:

- Ask questions.
- Make statements.
- Vote on all matters before the council.

During the meeting:

1. Bang your gavel to get everyone's attention and to call the City Council Meeting to order.

2. Follow this agenda.

   I.   Call the meeting to order

   II. Pledge of Allegiance

   III. Announcement from the City Clerk
        A. The Clerk gives instructions to the public on the procedure for speaking to the Council.

   IV. Announce the Purpose of the Meeting
        A. The purpose of this meeting is to make a decision on the proposed Lagoon Project.

   V.   Staff Reports
        A. Ask the City Planner to read the Description of the Project report.
        B. Ask the Environmental Planner to read the Environmental Impact Report.

   VI. Public Hearing
        A. Call on the Clerk to announce the names of people, one at a time, to come to the microphone. Speakers supporting the proposal will speak first.
        B. You should make sure speakers identify themselves and state whom they represent. Remind speakers to speak loudly and clearly so everyone can hear what they are saying.
        C. Each speaker is limited to 3 minutes. (Use a timer to monitor this procedure.)
        D. Use your gavel to maintain order. You may ask the Sergeant at Arms to remove anyone from the hearing who is disruptive or who refuses to be quiet.

   VII. Discussion and Vote on the Issue
        A. No one other than a City Council member may speak at this time. Remind members to speak loudly and clearly so all may hear.
        B. Explain to the Council members that it is up to them to decide what must be done about the proposed project. Ask Council Members what changes, if any, they would like to see in the project.
        C. Changes in the project may be proposed by any member of the Council and voted on.
        D. The Council may choose to accept the project as is, make changes, or reject the proposal.
        E. At the conclusion of the discussion, you must call for the vote and a decision must be made.

   VIII. Announcement of the Vote
        A. The City Clerk will call the names of the Council members in alphabetical order and ask them to vote "AYE" or "NAY." The Clerk will then announce the results to the public.

   IX. Adjourn
        A. Ask for a motion from the City Council to adjourn the meeting.

CITY CLERK WORKSHEET

You act as the Council secretary during the meeting. *Your responsibilities are:*

Before the City Council Meeting:

1. Make a voting record sheet which contains the names of the Council members in alphabetical order.

2. Get the "Request to Speak" cards from the Sergeant at Arms. Sort these into Support (FOR) and Oppose (AGAINST) groups. Write the names of the Speakers down on the Council Agenda. Give this to your teacher to copy for the City Council Meeting.

During the City Council Meeting:

1. Announcement from the Clerk—The President will ask you to tell the public that only those who have filled out a "Request to Speak" card will be allowed to speak during the meeting. Each person must wait until you call on them to speak. If anyone speaks without permission, the Sergeant at Arms will take them out of the room.

2. When the President asks you to, call each speaker, one at a time, up to speak. Announce each person's name loudly and clearly.

3. When it is time to vote, call the name of each Council member in alphabetical order and ask how that person votes: "AYE" or "NAY." Record each vote on your voting record sheet.

4. When the vote is finished, add up all of the votes and announce the results.

CITY COUNCIL MEETING AGENDA

Opening.. President
Pledge of Allegiance .... President
Announcement from City Clerk........................... City Clerk
Purpose of Meeting.. President

Read Description of the Project.......................... City Planner
Read Environmental Impact Report.................... Environmental Planner

PUBLIC HEARING

FOR (write in name of student speaker representing each group)

_____ Landowner

_____ Builder

_____ Business Owners

_____ Construction Workers

AGAINST (write in name of student speaker representing each group)

_____ Homeowners

_____ Bird Watchers Society

_____ Fishing Association

_____ PTA Parents

Purpose of Meeting.. President
Discussion and Vote on the Issue .... President
Announcement of the Vote .... City Clerk
Adjournment... President

113

Zoobooks®

SERGEANT AT ARMS WORKSHEET

You are a police officer. Your job is to keep order in the Council Meeting. *Your responsibilities are:*

Before the City Council Meeting:

1. Give one "Request to Speak" Card to each group listed on the agenda.

2. Collect all of the completed "Request to Speak" Cards and give them to the City Clerk.

During the City Council Meeting:

1. If anyone interrupts the President, City Clerk, or another speaker during the meeting, you will quietly ask that person to leave. (Check with the teacher to find out where the person should go.)

2. If ordered by the President, you will escort a troublesome person out of the Council room.

114

REQUEST TO SPEAK

_____
YOUR NAME

REQUEST TO SPEAK

_____
YOUR NAME

115

REQUEST TO SPEAK

_____
YOUR NAME

REQUEST TO SPEAK

_____
YOUR NAME

Zoobooks®

SPEAKING GROUPS PLANNING SHEET

FOR: Landowner
Builder
Business Owners
Construction Worker Association
Homeowners
Bird Watchers Society
Fishing Association
PTA Parents

Before the City Council Meeting:

116

1. Read your role card to understand your position.

2. Write a persuasive speech for the City Council Meeting. Explain why you are FOR or AGAINST the project and why the project would be helpful or harmful to the city.

3. If your group would like to change the plan, write how you would change the plan, and make a drawing to show your changes.

4. Elect a speaker for your group. Fill out a "Request to Speak" Card and give it back to the Sergeant at Arms.

During the City Council Meeting:

1. Listen to the ideas presented by other groups. When the City Clerk calls your speaker, he or she presents your group's speech.

FOR

The Lagoon Project

Landowner

You are the owner of the lagoon. You strongly support the project. You feel the land will be worth millions if the project goes through. If the land were set aside as a preserve for the least tern, you would lose a great deal of money. No one would want to buy a preserve. You feel you should have the right to do anything you want with the land you own.

AGAINST

The Lagoon Project

Homeowners

You are longtime residents of the area. You are against the project. Some of you have lived for over 50 years near the lagoon and enjoy views of its unspoiled beauty. You are against the project because the 10-story hotel will block your view. You are also concerned about the destruction of the shoreline and the trees that line it. You are worried that the least tern and other wildlife you enjoy watching will disappear.

FOR

The Lagoon Project

Builder

You have been hired by the owner of the property to build the project. You strongly support the project. You will tell the City Council that you plan to hire all the local workers you can find for the project. This will lower unemployment and bring money to the financially distressed city.

AGAINST

The Lagoon Project

Bird Watchers

You represent Citizens to Preserve the Least Tern, a local association with more than 300 members. You are against the project. You believe that the least tern desperately needs land for a breeding area. You firmly believe that if the proposal is approved, the number of least terns will decrease rapidly. You feel that the area is vital to the bird's survival. It would be a tragedy if the least tern were to become extinct.

117

FOR
The Lagoon Project

Business Owners

You are local business owners who own and operate your own businesses. You support the project. You feel it would help all businesses in the community by bringing tourists to the city. The tourists would spend their money in your local stores and in the community. Also, the workers building the project would spend money in the community.

AGAINST
The Lagoon Project

Fishing Association Member

You represent the local Fishing Association. You are against the project. You feel that building a road to the lagoon will be an invitation to more fishers, resulting in over-fishing and fewer fish in the lagoon, and more pedestrian visitors, resulting in damage to the natural shoreline. You also feel that the introduction of speedboats and water-skiers will disturb fish and pollute the lagoon, and that the addition of boat docks and beach areas will destroy the grassy shoreline. You believe the project will be harmful to the area and to your members.

FOR
The Lagoon Project

Construction Workers Association

You are construction workers. You support the project. Some of you have been out of work because of lack of new construction in your city. Unemployment is a real problem for many other people in your community, too. This project would provide hundreds of new jobs and increase prosperity for many.

AGAINST
The Lagoon Project

PTA Parents

You are parents of children who attend the school near the lagoon. You are against the project. You are worried that the new road the project will build will increase traffic in front of the school. This increased traffic could be dangerous when students are arriving at and departing from school.

You are also concerned that students will no longer be able to use the lagoon for field trips. Because of the construction, students will not be able to learn about the least tern and the aquatic environment. This valuable learning resource will be changed forever.

118

REPORTERS WORKSHEET

Before the City Council Meeting:

1. Decide in your group whom each of you will interview. One reporter could interview the City Council, another could interview the speakers, etc.

2. Write a list of questions you will ask the people you interview.

3. Conduct interviews and write up your first news article.

During the City Council Meeting:

1. Take notes during the meeting. Write down some quotes of statements made during the meeting to add to your story.

2. Write down the final decision and the number of "AYE" and "NAY" votes.

3. Work with your group to write an article on the City Council Meeting.

119

19
Looking for Responsible Solutions

Fill this Idea Web with ideas and facts about the technology your group is studying.

120

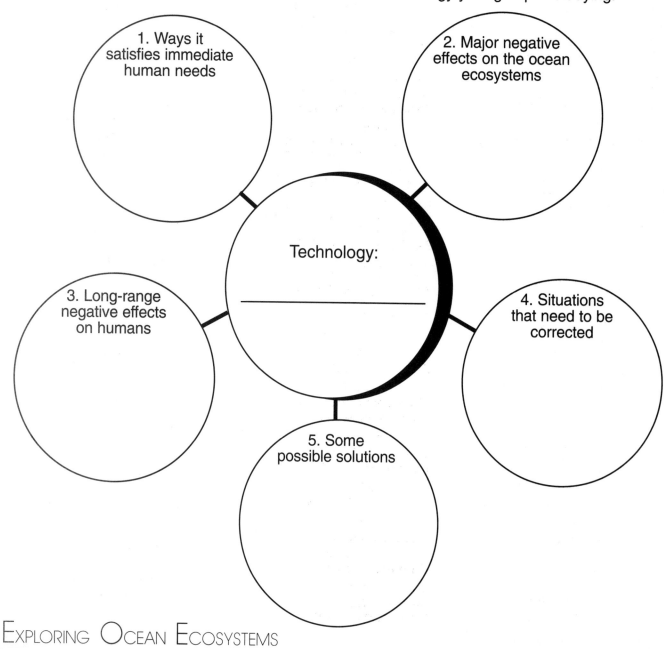

1. Ways it satisfies immediate human needs

2. Major negative effects on the ocean ecosystems

3. Long-range negative effects on humans

Technology:

_____

4. Situations that need to be corrected

5. Some possible solutions

BIBLIOGRAPHY

Animal Behaviors

Clarkson, Jan Nagel
Tricks Animals Play
National Geographic Society,
1975

Ferrell, Nancy Warren
Camouflage: Nature's Defense
Franklin Watts, Inc., 1989

Meyers, Arthur
*Sea Creatures Do
Amazing Things*
Random House, 1981

Oram, Liz
Migration in the Sea
Steck-Vaughn Library, 1992

Penny, Malcolm
Animal Camouflage
The Bookwright Press, 1988

Sibbald, Jean H.
Sea Creatures on the Move
Dillon Press, Inc., 1986

Art

Ames, Lee
*Draw 50 Sharks, Whales, and
Other Sea Creatures*
Doubleday, 1989

Careers in Oceanography

Paige, David
*A Day in the Life of a
Marine Biologist*
Troll Associates, 1981

Simon, Seymour
*How to be an Ocean Scientist
in Your Own Home*
J.B. Lippincott, 1988

Sipierg, Paul P.
I Can be an Oceanographer
Childrens Press, 1987

Diving

Ballard, Robert D.
Exploring the Titanic
Scholastic, 1988

McClung, Robert
Treasures in the Sea
National Geographic Society,
1972

McGovern, Ann
Night Dive
Macmillan, 1984

Tayntor, Elizabeth
Dive to the Coral Reefs
Crown Publishers, Inc., 1986

Environmental Conservation

Ancona, George
Turtle Watch
Macmillan, 1987

Bloyd, Sunni
Endangered Species
Lucent, 1989

Brown, Laurene Kraseny
*Dinosaurs to the Rescue:
A Guide to Protecting Our
Planet*
Joy Street Books, 1992

Gay, Kathlyn
Caretakers of the Earth
Enslow Publishers, 1993

Holms, Anita
*I Can Save the Earth: A Kid's
Handbook for Keeping Earth
Healthy and Green*
Julian Messner, 1993

Love, Ann
*Take Action: An Environmental
Book for Kids*
Tamborine Books, 1993

McVey, Vicki
*The Sierra Club Guide to
Planet Care and Repair*
Sierra Club Books for
Children, 1993

Markle, Sandra
The Kids' Earth Handbook
Atheneum, 1991

Taylor, David J.
Endangered Ocean Animals
Crabtree Publication Co., 1993

Tesar, Jenny E.
Threatened Oceans
Facts on File, 1991

Whitefield, Philip
Can the Whales Be Saved?
Viking Penguin, Inc., 1989

Wong, Ovid K.
Hands-On Ecology
Childrens Press, 1991

Yardley, Thompson
Make a Splash!
Millbrook Press, 1992

*E For Environment: An
Annotated Bibliography of
Children's Books with
Environmental Themes*
R.R. Bowker, 1992

*50 Simple Things Kids Can Do
to Save the Earth*
Andrews and McMeel, 1990

Kid Heroes of the Environment
Earth Works Press, 1991

Food Chains

Penny, Malcolm
The Food Chain
The Bookwright Press, 1988

Wolcott, Patty
Tunafish Sandwiches
Addison-Wessley, 1975

Human Uses of Ocean Resources

Brindeze, Ruth
*The Sea: The Story of the Rich
Underwater World*
Harcourt Brace Jovanovich,
1971

Fenton, D.X.
Harvesting the Sea
J. B. Lippincott, 1970

Fine, John Christopher
Oceans in Peril
Atheneum, 1987

Koch, Frances King
*Mariculture: Farming the
Fruits of the Sea*
Franklin Watts, Inc., 1992

Rayner, Ralph
Undersea Technology
The Bookwright Press, 1990

Literature

Aaron, Chester
Spill
Atheneum, 1977

Baker, Jeannie
*Where the Forest Meets the
Sea*
Greenwillow Books, 1988

Base, Graeme
*The Sign of the Seahorse:
A Tale of Greed and High
Adventure in Two Acts*
H.N. Abrams, 1992

Davis, Gibbs
Fisherman and Charley
Houghton Mifflin, 1983

Freeman, Don
The Seal and the Slick
Viking Press, 1974

George, Jean Craighead
The Talking Earth
HarperCollins, 1983

Moon, Pat
*Earthlines: Poems for the
Green Age*
Greenwillow Books, 1993

Orr, Katherine
My Grandpa and the Sea
Lerner/Carolrhoda, 1990

Savage, Deborah
Flight of the Albatross
Houghton Mifflin, 1989

Swanson, June
*That's for Shore:
Riddles from the Beach*
Lerner Publications Co., 1991

Thiele, Colin
Shadow Shark
HarperCollins, 1988

Weir, Ester
Action at Paradise Marsh
Stackpole Books, 1968

Oceans and Ocean Life

Baker, Lucy
Life in the Oceans
Franklin Watts, Inc., 1990

Barrett, Norman
Monsters of the Deep
Franklin Watts, Inc., 1991

Bender, Lionel
Life on a Coral Reef
Aladdin Books Ltd., 1989

Cole, Joanna
*The Magic School Bus on the
Ocean Floor*
Scholastic, 1992

Cook, David
Ocean Life
Crown Publishers, Inc., 1985

Doubilet, Anne
Under the Sea A to Z
Crown Publishers, Inc., 1991

Greenaway, Frank
Tide Pool
Dorling Kindersley, 1992

Hendrickson, Robert
The Ocean Almanac
Doubleday, 1984

Kaufman, Les
*Alligators to Zooplankton:
A Dictionary of Water Babies*
Franklin Watts, Inc., 1991

Markshak, Suzanna
I am the Ocean
Arcade Pub., 1991

Matthews, Rupert
Record Breakers of the Sea
Troll Associates, 1990

Sammon, Rick
*Seven Underwater
Wonders of the World*
Thomasson-Grant, 1992

Sibbald, Jean H.
Homes in the Sea
Dillon Press, Inc., 1986

Sibbald, Jean H.
Sea Babies
Dillon Press, Inc., 1986

Sibbald, Jean H.
Sea Mammals
Dillon Press, Inc., 1988

Simon, Seymour
Oceans
Morrow Junior Books, 1990

Animals at the Water's Edge
Raintree Publishers, 1987

Oceans
Time-Life Books, 1991

*The Random House Atlas of
the Oceans*
Random House, 1991

Videos and Films

*3-2-1 Contact, Program 14:
Flora and Fauna*
Childrens Television
Workshop, 1984 (Video)

*The Advance of
Science: Undersea*
Coronet, 1978 (Film)

The Earth: Its Oceans
Coronet, 1982 (Video and Film)

Endless Sea
Learning Corp. of America,
1974 (Film)

Gigi's Legacy
Bernnett Marine Video, 1989
(Video)

Hide and Seek
Oxford Scientific Films, 1986
G.P. Putnam's Sons (Film)

The Living Ocean
National Geographic, 1988
(Video)

Plankton to Fish: A Food Cycle
Coronet, 1975 (Film)

Riches from the Sea
National Geographic, 1984
(Video)

*Strange and Unusual Animals:
Adaptations to Environment*
AIMS Education Foundation,
1974 (Video and Film)

The Voyage of the Mimi
Bank Street College of
Education, 1984 (Video)